MUSICIANS INSTITUTE

ESSENTIAL CONCEPTS

Advanced VOCAL TECHNIQUE

Middle Voice, Placement & Style

**By Dena Murray
and Tita Hutchison**

ISBN 978-0-634-09497-2

HAL•LEONARD® CORPORATION

7777 W. BLUEMOUND RD. P.O. BOX 13819 MILWAUKEE, WI 53213

In Australia Contact:
Hal Leonard Australia Pty. Ltd.
4 Lentara Court
Cheltenham, Victoria, 3192 Australia
Email: ausadmin@halleonard.com.au

Visit Hal Leonard Online at
www.halleonard.com

Table of Contents

Introduction

A voice that sounds like one register: isn't this what most singers want? And, if you weren't born with that natural gift, then you probably sought out instruction from voice teachers to fix what feels weak and pitchy, or where your voice breaks. Many of you want your voice to sound like a big chest voice throughout the entire range because, when listening to your favorite singers, that's what it sounds like—a chest voice that keeps going higher and higher. What you don't know is that, even though it is a chest-like sound, it isn't being sung with the chest register alone. When listening to CDs, we often forget what goes on in the studio. Engineers make that singer sound better by adding reverb, compression, special mixing techniques, auto-tune, or even voice doubling.

So, if you can't build a voice on chest voice alone, then how do you get it to sound like that? And, how do you get it to sound like that *live*, outside of all the engineering tools used in a studio? If you can naturally achieve such a sound without straining, then what are you doing? What makes it right when it's right? How do you know when it's wrong, or when you could be hurting yourself and not even know it? Has your style of singing become such a habit that it feels more comfortable to keep singing *that* way than it does to change it? How is the mechanism of the human voice supposed to work and still sound *good*? How can you get power into your voice, bridge all the breaks, correct pitch, and have the entire instrument sound like one register instead of two?

First, your voice must have a good foundation. This means that you must fully develop both your chest and head registers before working to bring them together and bridge the middle. Otherwise, the problems that you currently experience will remain problems when you try to bridge the breaks and achieve a well-balanced sound. Without proper development, you put yourself at risk for manipulating your voice in unnatural ways: using your body, neck muscles, and abdominal muscles to help you reach notes when the vocal cord mechanism itself should be doing this work for you. You shouldn't have to physically struggle with your body to pop out notes and have them sound the way you want them to sound.

For those who weren't born with a naturally gifted voice, the good news is that you can learn how to sing well. Getting the voice bridged, working on the middle range, and getting the sound you desire for the style in which you prefer to sing are *all* learned skills. It's not impossible, but it does require a great deal of patience and per-sistence—a relentless determination to have your voice perform the way you dream to hear it.

And for those who can already sing well, it's important to educate yourselves about your instrument. Otherwise, you put your voice at risk for acquiring bad habits later on—habits that can damage your throat if you don't understand what you are doing, how it is that you do it, and what makes *your* voice such a gift.

SECTION I:
BUILDING A FOUNDATION
A Quick Refresher on Musical Terms: Scale, Key, Octave, etc.

Before we start building our foundation, let's revisit a few terms that you may or may not be familiar with. These are musical terms that will be useful in navigating this book.

Scale: The term *scale*, in this book, refers to vocal exercises—that is, a series of notes in a particular order and pattern.*

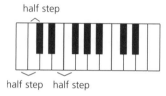

Key: When we practice a scale, we'll sing it in different *keys*. This will allow us to cover our entire voice range. Each scale will be sung once, then moved up or down by a half step and sung again in the next key, and so on. (On the piano, a *half step* is the distance from one note to the next adjacent note.)

Octave: An *octave* is the distance from one note name to the same note name 12 notes apart (for example, from C to C).

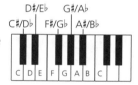

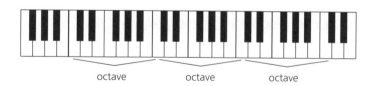

Middle C: To keep track of their range, many vocalists find it helpful to orient themselves to an instrument such as piano or guitar. In particular, you should be aware of the location of middle C—this is the C found just left of center on a full piano keyboard. This note will be given the name C1. Other C notes located higher and lower than that will be numbered accordingly.

middle C on a guitar

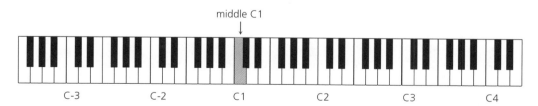

*In general music terminology, the word *scale* often denotes something slightly different: a set of pitches that define a particular quality or tonality—like major, minor, diminished, etc. That is not the meaning intended here. All the scales in the book are based on a major tonality.

How Your Voice Works

The *vocal cords* are two flexible ligaments that lie right beside one another and are no more than an inch in length. They are attached to two main muscle and cartilage groups that help the cords stretch from front to back—not side to side. The vocal cords must make a new adjustment for every single pitch. Many singers are unaware of this and usually seek to hit the higher pitches of songs with the reach of their air, but this only puts intense strain on the vocal cords and, over time, can cause damage.

There are many different names for all the muscles and cartilages that make up the vocal cord mechanism. This can get very confusing when trying to explain only what you need to know. For simplicity's sake, we have chosen to break all these names down by lumping them together into two main muscle groups: the *thyroid group* (right behind the Adam's apple at the front of the larynx), and the *arytenoid group* (located at the back of the larynx).

Thyroid and Arytenoid Groups
(as if looking down the throat)

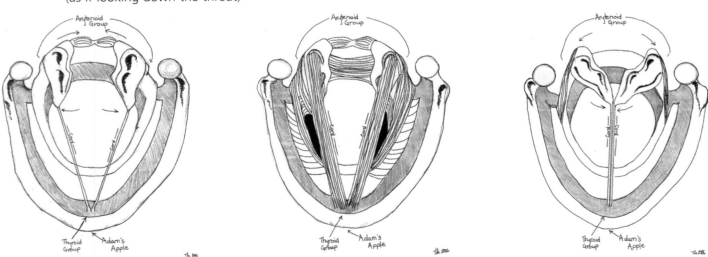

The arytenoids group releasing tension (left), relaxed (middle), and tightening the vocal cords (right).

The thyroid group is primarily associated with the lower register (or chest voice). The arytenoid group is primarily associated with the upper register (or head voice) mostly because of how that group of muscles and cartilage continues to stretch backwards the higher in pitch you go (the thyroid group holds in a V-grip position to act as bracing tension for the arytenoids as they stretch back).

The higher you go, the farther the arytenoid group stretches back, while the thyroid group holds fairly steady. The larynx will rock up and down just a tiny bit (a quarter of an inch or less) as you sing through your registers, but for the most part, it should stay centered. It should not be moving upward by a half inch or more the higher you go, nor should it push downwards by a half inch or more the lower you go.

If the thyroid group stays in the correct position, then the arytenoids should be able to take varying weights of the cords themselves as they stretch farther and farther back for the highest notes. This means the chest voice will thin but will still sound like a chest voice because the arytenoids will be able to use the thyroid group as bracing tension as the cords stretch backwards for every higher pitch. When the cords, muscles, and cartilage work in this way, the upper-middle register is able to retain what sounds like a chest voice. However, it's important to understand that using the chest voice alone does not create the chest voice sound; the arytenoids must be working, too.

MIDDLE OF THE VOICE

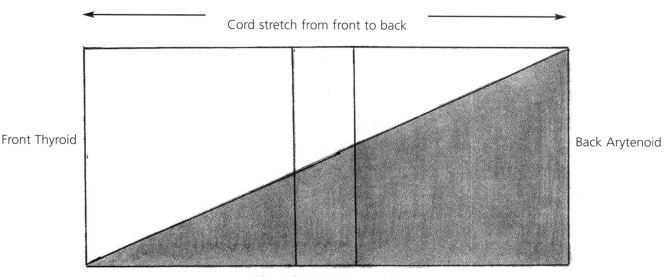

Cord stretch from front to back

Front Thyroid

Back Arytenoid

Thyroid 50/50 Arytenoid

Arytenoids must start stretching on the lowest notes and keep stretching further back for each successively higher note.

Thyroid group holds firm in a V-grip position to act as bracing tension for arytenoids when they stretch.

Note: if arytenoids aren't working in the low voice, they won't hold their strength through the middle and this will cause you to "break."

To feel the thyroid group in action, put your finger on your larynx where the Adam's apple is, and start talking (*see below*). As you begin to speak, you should feel that part of your throat vibrating. As you take your voice higher and higher in pitch, you should feel the Adam's apple move up and backwards a little bit, but it should not be jumping up. If you feel it jumping up about a half of an inch or more, it means you're either squeezing or pushing with the neck and stomach muscles. (Note: the Adam's apple is much more pronounced in men than it is in women. This is due to hormones. However, there are some women who may have a more pronounced Adam's apple. If you can't find the apple, place your finger somewhere in the middle of your larynx and keep talking until you feel where it is vibrating most.)

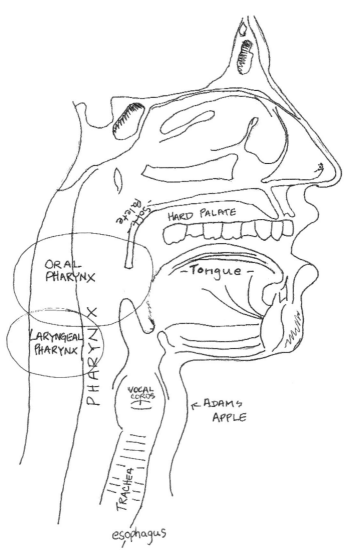

Singing with a voice that sounds like one register has been labeled many things: full voice, bridged voice, middle voice, pharyngeal voice, the mix, or the blend. What these terms really mean is that you are using the entire vocal cord mechanism when singing—both the arytenoid and thyroid groups together. It's not just one group alone that makes all of this happen correctly.

Air Function and Placement

The two most important factors in voice are *air function* and *placement*. If the voice is not properly placed or the air is not flowing, you will have to squeeze, tighten the neck muscles, and push up with the stomach muscles just to get sound out. Resorting to these measures only distorts the sound and creates more problems.

Air Function

To sing well, the cords have to be able to control the flow of air, and the air must be flowing. Sound is produced when the air strikes the cords. Since this is the case, if you squeeze and tighten your neck and stomach muscles so much that no air can pass between the cords, you will be forced to push your air up with your stomach muscles and blow air between the cords just to get the sound to come out. To avoid this harmful setup, you may need to work on your breathing pattern. If your breathing pattern is fine, then your next step is learning how to properly place the voice for any given style of singing.

Placement

Placement is not only about familiarizing yourself with all the correct feelings and sensations of "singing in the mask" (sound resonating as it *reaches* the front of the face), but also familiarizing yourself with any bad habits that are getting in the way. Without knowing, sensing, and feeling both right and wrong placement, you won't be able to get your cords to stretch properly and control the flow of air.

Working on the Breathing Pattern

The Diaphragm Supports without Pushing

The diaphragm supports your vocal cords by automatically expanding, and it is supposed to stay out while the cords (not you or your body) take control of the flow of air until the air finally runs out. It can't do that if you are blowing all your air out with your stomach pushing up or punching in your stomach to push the note out. These faulty techniques will actually make the diaphragm collapse.

So "expanding outwardly" when singing does not mean tensing the diaphragm to push it out and keep it out. If the cords are able to control the flow of air, the diaphragm will stay out automatically. This is why the diaphragm is referred to as the supporting mechanism. When the diaphragm expands outwardly in a natural way, it literally supports the column of air. Supported properly, the cords can act as a valve and platform. This natural outward expansion of support permits the cords to take over by stretching across the top of the column of air and compressing it.

Let the Vocal Cords Control the Flow of Air

You shouldn't have to try to hang onto your air for fear you won't have enough. If the cords are controlling the flow, you should have plenty. With air, it's a good idea to think "less is more," because the cords only need a small amount of air to compress it and control it (unless you need to take more in and blow more out for a stylistic effect).

Holding your breath to eke out a little air at a time only creates a lot of pressure under the cords, forcing them to pull further apart when you begin singing, because they can't control too much air pressure. If there is too much air sitting underneath them, when you start singing, they will have to release some—if not most—of it, as soon as you start. Once this happens, it makes you think that you didn't take in enough air to begin with and that you probably need to take in even more on your next try.

So, you go after it again, only this time your thinking tells you that you must fill up your stomach with as much air as you possibly can. As soon as you do this, you find out that the result is exactly the same as the last time you tried it—you lost all your air at once. There still wasn't enough to take you through the exercise or phrase. Additionally, filling up and holding your breath in this way only makes you feel like you can't breathe!

The Vocal Cords and Diaphragm Work Together

When you take in air through the mouth (as you should), the vocal cords open for it, and they close as soon as that air has been taken in. You could say the vocal cords are like a valve, because of this opening and closing action that takes place. If you think about it, there is no such place within the diaphragm—no such valve where you can say, "Only this much air should come through at this time." Doing that would mean trying to control the air by either holding your breath, squeezing it, or tensing the stomach muscles in some way. Remember, the air has to be flowing at a natural rate of speed. You shouldn't have to manipulate and control any part of your body just to get notes out. Because the cords open and close like a valve, they are the only part of the singing anatomy that can really take control of the column of air, and it is one of their functions to do so.

What happens between the cords and the breath is supposed to be a simultaneous action. The cords can't work without the breath, and the breath can't work without the cords. You can't start one without the other. Most people are very aware that the diaphragm is supposed to work to support the tone. What they are unaware of is *how the cords* are supposed to be controlling the flow of air. If the cords can't control what happens, you may get pitchy or lose all your air before you get to the end of a phrase, and/or you will have to strain by squeezing and tensing your neck muscles just to hold onto that air while trying to make your way through a phrase.

It's Not Just About the Diaphragm

The diaphragm creates a lot of controversy. Many vocal instructors can hear when the cords are not properly controlling the flow of air. They will offer diaphragmatic techniques in an effort to try to get the diaphragm to support the tone, and subsequently get the cords to stretch properly. Singers often misinterpret what the instructor is trying to accomplish by introducing these techniques. It's usually not the "in" action instructors are trying to get you to perform; it's the "out" action they are trying to get you to practice *without tensing* the stomach to keep the diaphragm pushed out. To maintain the platform-like effect of the cords, the diaphragm must be expanding outwardly and staying out naturally as the cords control and compress the air. But because of misinterpretation or poor communication skills, focusing on lots of abdominal and diaphragmatic techniques doesn't always fix the problem and can often create even more of them. Sometimes it leads singers into squeezing the neck, pushing up the stomach muscles, and holding the breath, which again, over time, can cause damage.

Airflow Exercises

There is a good possibility that anyone who has a problem with his or her air flow has a problem with the breathing pattern. A large percentage of singers trying to straighten out problems with their voice resort to using the diaphragm primarily, as if their voice box were located somewhere inside of it. Remember it is not the breath or amount of air you use that is responsible for each pitch or even the sound. The breath is only responsible for taking the sound out of you. It is the vocal cords that control and create each and every pitch, and once the air strikes those cords, there is sound. This is why the air is often referred to as the *propelling* mechanism while the cords are often referred to as the *producing* mechanism.

The following exercises will help if you need to re-train the way you use your diaphragm/breath/air.

Pushing Exercise: Descending and Ascending Scale with Glottal Attack

Many singers will resort to pushing up the stomach muscles when trying to reach the higher notes of a song. This is because it's much easier to feel the power of your breath than it is anything else; because the breath is so powerful, you're pretty sure you *can* reach higher notes with it. Yet, a problem still remains. When using the breath this way, you can't really gauge how the notes will sound when they come out, or even if you'll hit them. Unless it's used for an effect, using too much air (or "filling up the tank") often distorts the tone. In many cases the sound is not what you were looking for on those notes and feels uncontrollable.

To help eliminate pushing up the stomach muscles, try using a glottal attack. The attack begins with the cords coming together, closing the opening between them (known as the *glottis*). It's a slight stroke of the cords that feels and sounds a little bit like the cords are slightly "biting" one another just before the actual sound is produced. If you're doing it wrong, you will feel your diaphragm and stomach jerking in or pushing upward to make this sound. When you're doing it right, if you put your fingers on your Adam's apple, you will feel the vibration of the attack right behind it, and the diaphragm and stomach will not be punching in or up.

The following exercise should help you to stop blowing too much air through your vocal cords. Blowing too much air will result in the cords not being capable of controlling the flow. If you end up not having enough air to get you through a scale or phrase, you may be squeezing the cords so tightly with your neck muscles that they are slammed shut inside and holding your breath. Squeezing the cords shut and holding the breath will only force you to blow out more air for sound. Check to make sure you are not doing either of these things and try again.

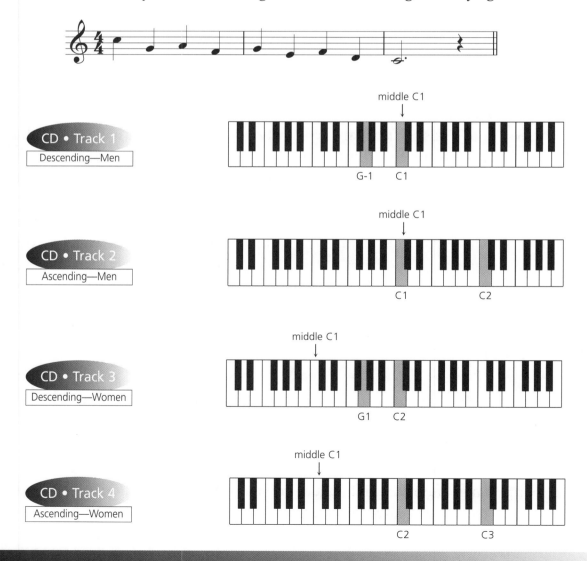

Squeezing Exercise: Descending and Ascending Scale with an "H"

Similarly to pushing, squeezing usually occurs when singers are trying to mask their break or to get more edge in their sound. When you squeeze your stomach and neck muscles, you keep the air from passing through the cords. Remember: sound cannot be created unless air strikes the cords. So if you're squeezing because you want more edge—and instinctively know that you can't get air to pass through the cords because of it—you will most likely resort to punching in your stomach muscles to push air up through the cords. Squeezing forces you to push. It is the most injurious of all the bad habits you can have because the cords are constantly rubbing together and air is constantly blasting through. Once the air blasts through, the cords slam back together. If you consistently do this for style, it may become a habit and a vicious cycle that, over time, will create damage.

To help you stop squeezing, try adding a slight "H" to the first note. However, some singers get carried away with the "H" and start pronouncing the "H" from their stomachs, consequently blowing way too much air out at once. We suggest you attack the "H" very slightly, as if the "H" is actually created from the back of your throat (straight at the back of your mouth), rather than from down below in your gut. It shouldn't be a big HUH—more like an implied "H" that feels like it starts on that back wall using just a small amount of air (performing this exercise by starting out as if you are *speaking* the "H," rather than singing it, may help).

Air should not be the first thing you hear before sound starts coming out. The air and sound should start together, and it should feel as if the sound itself (which is the cords) is taking control of that air and compressing it while the air continues to carry the sound out of you. You really have to concentrate when doing this because it is too easy to involve the neck and stomach muscles.

If you have been squeezing out of habit for a long time, this exercise can be difficult. It requires a good deal of visualizing and concentration, because you cannot push the air through the cords by using the stomach with a big HUH. It has to be a gentle "H" that starts from above, as if coming from somewhere at the back of the head (back wall of the throat, inside the mouth) and not from below (way down in the stomach).

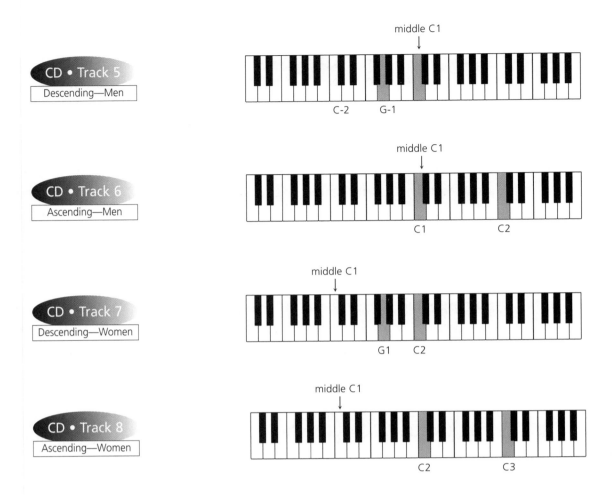

CD • Track 5
Descending—Men

middle C1

C-2   G-1

CD • Track 6
Ascending—Men

middle C1

C1   C2

CD • Track 7
Descending—Women

middle C1

G1   C2

CD • Track 8
Ascending—Women

middle C1

C2   C3

Exercising the Tongue and Mouth

The Tongue

The tongue is often referred to as the worst enemy of the singer. Singers often tense it and use the swallowing muscles (underneath the chin and attached to the tongue) when trying to attain sounds they don't know how to create or even imitate. Unless it's for an effect, doing this on a consistent basis can add strain to the voice, cause you to choke on the tone, and leave you with the feeling (and sound) that it is trapped in the back somewhere.

Don't Flatten the Tongue Too Much

The tongue is a huge muscle. The only part of it that we ever really see when we look in the mirror is the top part of it and the attachment directly underneath it, but the tongue muscle actually goes all the way underneath your chin and more than halfway down your throat (*see the diagram on page 8*). It's as big as a fist. So if you flatten it too much, you can see how this might force the back of it to push down and backwards, pushing the epiglottis back and down so that it closes the lower portion of the pharynx/tube.

Flattening the tongue can also squish it down so much that it has to push down on those swallowing muscles under the chin, forcing those muscles to tense or protrude out. This is what makes the voice sound as if it is trapped, or even garbled. Even if the singer has the tongue in one of the two suggested tongue positions (which we'll focus on in the next section), it's still possible that the tongue may be lying too flat.

Singers who flatten their tongue too much will often complain that their sound is choked off and feels strained—especially under the back part of the jaw on both sides the neck. If you are one of these people, you must try to raise the back of your tongue up a little bit, yet still keep it as relaxed as possible so that the pharynx/tube stays open.

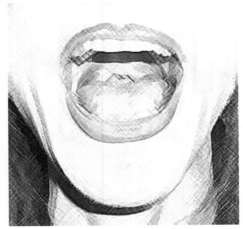

Flattened tongue will cause soft palate to pull down, close tube, and trap sound.

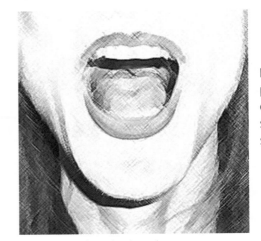

Notice how soft palate raises and opens from side to side (expansion of soft palate).

Tongue too flat—Improper position

Raised and relaxed tongue—proper position

Watch your tongue in a mirror so you can see if you are flattening it too much. Some vowels are easier to work with than others, and the problem won't be as bad on those vowels. AH is a notoriously bad vowel for people with this problem. Everyone seems to want to flatten his or her tongue from side to side when pronouncing this vowel.

Two Suggested Tongue Positions

There are two suggested tongue positions to help you get your tongue under control. The size of your tongue will dictate which position is best for you. You'll probably have to try both to make that decision.

If your tongue is small enough, put the tip right behind the back of your lower front teeth. If you tend to pull your tongue backwards as you are singing, you end up trapping the sound in the tube, rather than allowing it to easily come up and out. Putting the tip right behind the lower front teeth and keeping it there while you are exercising or singing songs will help free the voice.

The second position is to lay your tongue right on top of the lower front teeth. This often makes singers feel as if they are singing with their tongue hanging out. But remember: this is for exercise and to break the habit of having the tongue in the way. It is extremely important that you learn how to do this for an open sound. If your tongue takes up your whole mouth by putting it behind your lower front teeth, then you will have to use this second position.

In both cases, it's very important to keep the tongue and swallowing muscles as relaxed as possible. Since the tongue is a muscle, it is attached to other muscles. This can mean that, when the tongue pulls back, it might not just push down on the epiglottis, it may also pull back the arches of the soft palate (*see diagram on page 8*). If the soft palate pulls backwards, it will close the upper portion of the pharynx/tube creating a nasal sound. Since the pharynx/tube is responsible for resonance, it's very important that this tube (from the bottom to the top) remains open and free of interference.

The Mouth

The mouth should never open too wide or too tall. To get a good position for the mouth, sit with a mirror. Stick two fingers in your mouth (or the circumference of a cork) and this will give you the approximate size for the opening. Then relax your jaw so it doesn't feel or look stiff. Smile a little bit.

When exercising the voice on AH, EH, and EE, the mouth shape should stay the same and the jaw should not move:

Mouth position on AH/EH/EE

On OH, the lips will help shape the OH, but the mouth should remain just as open:

Mouth position on OH

On OO, the lips will come in to shape this vowel even more, but again, the mouth should stay open while the jaw moves ever so slightly (but not so much that your mouth ends up closing).

Mouth position on OO

When singing songs, these same rules apply—except that the jaw will have to move considerably more than it does to exercise on vowels alone because now you are forming words by using the consonants and articulators (the tongue, teeth, lips, and palate). However, your mouth should never be tight-lipped and closing even when singing songs (unless you are doing this for an effect). If the mouth is too tight and closing, the sound will not come out well. Try to sing with your mouth in the position shown below, and don't be afraid to use your face to help with the position.

Proper mouth position when singing and using "mask" placement

If you have ever watched some of your favorite singers, you've probably noticed the strange faces they make, especially the good singers. Those faces aren't so much about passion as they are about technique. They use their face as another way to help brace the sound in the mask for placement. So you can't be afraid to look ugly. They sure aren't.

Exercise: Breaking the Habit of Using the Tongue and Swallowing Muscles (54321)

To help you stop using your tongue and swallowing muscles, first open your mouth. (Remember, the mouth should open up to about the width of two fingers.) Put your tongue in one of the two positions suggested, and then relax your tongue and jaw while staying in that open position. Make sure the muscles from the tongue (under the chin) are not protruding out or tightening.

To check for tightening muscles under the chin, put your finger under your chin (in the middle, under the chin) and swallow. When you swallow you can feel the muscle move. This muscle should *not* be moving when you exercise your voice and sing, so checking with your finger under the chin should help—especially if you have this problem.

Once everything is in position and relaxed, start singing this exercise on the vowel AH. Make sure that nothing moves as you come down the scale—not your tongue, mouth, or jaw. Everything should remain exactly the same from the moment you start that first note to the time you finish the last.

Do this full two-octave exercise (the lowest note for men is C-1, and for women it's G-1) with *only* the tongue in mind. *Do not* listen to the sound. At this point, it really doesn't matter what you sound like. The idea is to *break the habit* of using the tongue incorrectly. Look into a mirror to check and see if your tongue is pulling back or flattening. And use your fingers to feel the muscles on the underside of your chin to see if they are tightening or protruding out. If you know you have a problem with your tongue, you may have to work like this for a week or more.

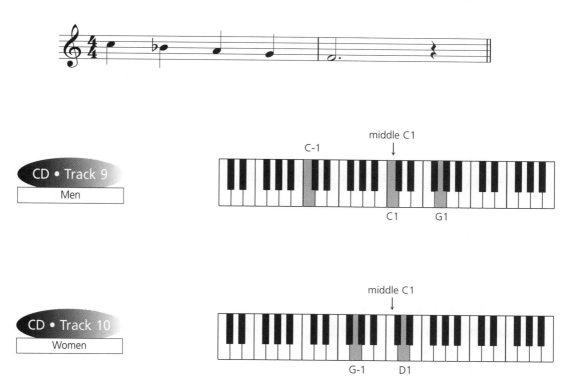

CD • Track 9
Men

CD • Track 10
Women

As an exercise, when singing songs it's a good idea to try to sing with the tongue forward, making sure you always feel it at your teeth. If you don't feel it at your teeth on every word, it may be pulling back. Use a mirror if you have to. Again, this is not about how you sound, so try not to listen. Instead, concentrate on keeping that tongue forward while singing.

If you know you have tongue problems, this habit may occasionally resurface, so make sure to monitor it. If you tape your exercises and songs, you may hear when your sound gets trapped or nasal. If you do hear this, there is a good chance that your tongue and/or swallowing muscles have gotten in the way again. That will be your cue to get back to work!

Feeling Your Voice

Feeling the Cords

Our experience has shown us that the greatest success in achieving the voice you want comes not from overemphasizing the diaphragm, but from sensing how to feel your cords and, subsequently, feeling the sound and its placement as it comes into the mask. This ability comes from recognizing and feeling what you've been doing wrong. Because many things become habits, the habits will always feel more comfortable. If you've been doing something a certain way for a long time, it will feel much more comfortable to go back to your bad habit than it will to try to change it by doing it a different way. It's not until you *physically experience* the right way enough times that you begin to recognize what you've been doing wrong and just how uncomfortable that way of singing really is.

Contrary to what a lot of people think, it is possible to feel the cords if you are given the right instructions.

Exercise for Feeling the Cords

Let's start by humming. Humming loudly engages the cords, so hum loudly on any note of your choosing, and *listen to the sound* of that hum. Try to feel exactly where the hum is originating. You should feel it coming from somewhere inside the middle of your neck. Try to hold the hum as long as you can. (Some people are surprised at how long they can hold a hum.) Once you're holding the hum, check to see if you are doing anything with your diaphragm to keep the hum going. You should only feel the diaphragm moving in when you're running out of breath; most of the time, you should not have had to do anything, and the diaphragm should stay out (without tensing the muscles in any way to stay out).

The sound of your hum *is* the stretch of your cord. That stretch literally controls the flow of air, which is a chief responsibility of the cords when phonating and singing. If the cords are doing their job, you should have air left over by the time you reach the end of an exercise. If the cords are not controlling the flow, you will feel as if you don't have enough air and must resort to manipulating your stomach and neck muscles in an effort to keep the air going. Remember: you should not have to control the flow of air with your body in any way.

Working with Vowels

Since the actual *sound* of the voice is given by vowels, correct pronunciation of them will help place the voice in its natural physiological center. Italian is the only existing language in which the vowels are physiologically formed correctly; they are larger in shape, more resonant, and fuller in volume than the vowels of other languages. Therefore, these are the vowels we'll use when working with the exercises.

In English, the five vowel classifications are I, E, A, O, U. In Italian these same vowels are pronounced as: EE (as in the word "feet"), EH (as in the word "they"), AH (as in the word "father"), OH (as in the word "go"), and OO (as in the word "food"). From here on out we will refer to these vowels exactly as we have phonetically sounded and spelled them out. (Note: This does not reflect the international phonetic alphabet. We have chosen this way of spelling out the vowels because it has proven to be easier for most people to learn when training the voice.)

Feeling the Direction of Air

A lot of people think the vowels are formed in the mouth, because they feel air in the mouth. What they're actually feeling here is the *direction of air* created by the vowel. Vowels are formed somewhere between the laryngeal and oral pharynx (*see diagram on page 8*).

Each vowel creates its own direction of air because each vowel has its own unique shape. To get an idea of what this feels like, let's start with the vowel EE (as in the word "feet"). Say it aloud a few times. See if you can feel the air from the EE strike right behind the upper front teeth. It might take a few tries before you can feel it. (If you can't feel the air behind the teeth, try closing your mouth, as if you are saying "cheese" to the camera, and say EE again. You should feel the air, and vibration, striking behind the upper front teeth.)

Next, try the vowel EH (as in the word "they"). Say it aloud a few times and see if you can feel the air from the EH striking the front of the hard palate. Say EE, then EH consecutively; you should feel the EH move a little further back than where you felt the EE.

For the vowel AH (as in the word "father"), the mouth opens and the tongue lies fairly flat compared to that of the other vowels, though the underside of the tongue should not be tensing to flatten. When you say AH you should feel the air from the AH going straight up the middle of the hard palate. Now say EE, then EH, then AH consecutively and see if you can feel the air moving a little further back with each new vowel sound as you switch from vowel to vowel. You should feel the air move from its starting point on EE (right behind the teeth) to its ending point on AH (which is felt at the middle of the hard palate)—as if the direction of air on AH is now vertical. If you're not feeling it, keep doing it until you do.

On OH (as in the word "go"), you should feel a subtle movement of air on a diagonal from the front of the soft palate to the top of your head (or thereabouts). Say EE, EH, AH, OH consecutively and see if you can feel the movement from vowel to vowel as it starts from right behind the front teeth on EE and ends on the diagonal with OH.

Lastly, on OO (as in the word "food") you should feel the air moving from the back of the throat to the front of the mouth. Now say EE, EH, AH, OH, OO consecutively and see if you can feel the direction of air moving from where it starts on EE (behind the front teeth) and ends on OO (which is all the way at the back of the mouth by the time you get to this vowel sound). If you have a problem pronouncing OO, try saying "EW" ("EW" as if someone just told you something disgusting) and see if you can feel the OO part of that word.

Feeling Where the Vowel Is Formed

To get an idea of how to feel where the vowels themselves are actually formed, try to focus your attention inwardly, to the cavity where the vowel should begin shaping. Again, the pharynx is the resonance chamber, and the vowels are shaped somewhere between the laryngeal and oral part of that tube (*see diagram on page 8*). If you are unclear about exactly where to concentrate, get a mirror. Drop your head back a little and take a look at the back of your throat in the mirror. You will see the uvula, which looks similar to a punching bag and hangs down from the top of the soft palate. Now, relax your throat by dropping your larynx and say AH. You should see open space in the front of, and back of, the uvula and a hole right behind the tongue (which is actually the beginning of the pharynx). It's all the surrounding muscles of that tube (the pharynx) that shape each vowel.

Shape Vowels in the Pharynx, *Not* with the Vocal Cords

When working with the exercises and songs, it is extremely important that vowels take shape in the pharynx and not with the vocal cords and tightening neck muscles. The reason so many singers have trouble with vowels like EE, AH, and OO is because they try to pronounce those vowels down inside the throat by squeezing the vocal cords together.

You must use all your effort to concentrate on feeling the *shaping* of the vowel in the oral pharynx and the sound and air (resonance) as traveling to the front of the face (like it's riding on a wire from the back of the head to the front of the face). On the lowest notes, this resonance is felt moving toward the front of the hard palate, just behind the nose—not inside of it. As you get higher in pitch, the vowel should feel as if it starts shaping just above the soft palate and all of its surrounding area, and the resonance should move higher up with it—behind the nose. Again, it should not be felt inside the nose (otherwise it may feel tight and nasal, and sound nasal).

It's a mind trick to think of the sound starting at the back of your head, rather than from inside the neck. As you produce sound, use your mind to sense the resonance as it travels along a line from the back of your head toward the front of your face.

Even if the exercise is a descending exercise, don't visualize the notes as they descend or the low notes will begin to drop under the chin, possibly lower than the larynx, and you might start getting pitchy. If you *can* visualize notes moving straight along on that line from the back of your head to the front of your face, you may feel a big difference. It shouldn't feel strained, and your vowels shouldn't feel stuck or trapped in the back of your throat.

If you *do* feel strain or if your vowels get trapped in the back of your throat, then you are probably squeezing with your neck muscles or pushing in and up with your stomach muscles. In this case, work towards breaking this habit by learning how to get that air to feel like it starts from above (the back wall of the throat from inside the mouth and at the back of your head)—and not from somewhere below (like the stomach). The higher up you go, the higher up at the back of the head you should be imagining and visualizing the starting point. The trick is to *use* your air; feel it in the tube as it comes up to propel the sound out *without* blowing it up from your stomach to accomplish this.

Sing from the Neck Up

Speech-level singing takes place from the neck up. All talking and singing should begin by using the upper portion of the pharynx (oral pharynx), which is at the back of the throat inside the mouth. The higher you go, the sound (resonance) moves from mouth level (on the lowest notes) to behind the nose, then into the cheeks and to eye level and, on the highest notes, maybe even into the forehead.

Using your mind in this way will help you keep the back of your throat open. It is only through your ability to visualize that this will happen; there isn't anything you can do physically to make these things happen. Take control of your mind and direct it by telling yourself what to feel, where, and how to do it.

The soft palate will often feel as if it is expanding from side to side when you've done it correctly, and the sound will feel easy, free, and resonant. Again, there isn't anything physical you can do to get that soft palate to expand from side to side. The more you visualize and think about it, the more you will begin to sense it.

Exercise for Feeling Where the Vowels are Formed

This exercise will help you feel where the vowels actually start taking shape, rather than where you feel the direction of air in the mouth. Taking the vowels EE, EH, AH, OH, OO consecutively, sing them on one pitch—any pitch—all in one breath. Try not to move your jaw when performing this exercise. (You can keep from moving the jaw by placing your index fingers on either side of it to remind you not to move it.)

Next, focus on feeling those vowels take shape inside the tube on the back wall of the throat, straight back from the front of your mouth (oral pharynx area). If you can't sense or feel the sound there, keep visualizing it starting there or use a mirror to look. It may take a few tries before you actually feel where that shape is taking place. It may require a *lot* of visualizing and focusing your mind on that part of your throat.

Resonance and the Resonance Chambers

The body works like an acoustic instrument, and there are a few places where you can feel sound resonating in the body. For example, if you look at an acoustic guitar, it has a hollow body with a round hole in the middle. When you strum, the sound bounces around the inside of that body, is magnified, and then amplified through the opening. That magnification is known as resonance.

Unlike the guitar, the voice has a variety of places inside the human body where it can resonate. Those places include the chest cavity, the mouth (hard and soft palate), the sinus cavity, and very high up in the head.

As stated earlier, resonance is created in the tube known as the pharynx (*see diagram on page 8*). It carries the sound and airwaves into the cavities of the head. When the sound and the airwaves travel into these cavities free of interference, they will vibrate against them. The pharynx is often referred to as the *echo chamber* because when the sound and air (resonance) move into the facial and head cavities and vibrate against them, the "mask" then acts as an amplifier. True loudness is properly achieved with these three things: vibration of the cord, resonance, and correct voice placement.

SECTION II: MIDDLE VOICE AND PLACEMENT

Always Remember This

We are about to embark on a journey to bridge the voice, fix all the breaks, work through your middle range, get the voice to sound like one register, and learn how to strengthen the voice.

Exercising the voice is *always* going to be hard work—much harder than singing songs—because, when exercising, you will constantly strive to get it perfect. However, on any given day, your voice may not be going to the right places. Whether it's the food you ate, the way you are feeling physically or emotionally, or a variety of other reasons, it's important to understand that your voice lives inside of your body and is affected by everything you think, feel, do, and eat.

Keeping these things in mind, the voice will *never* be perfect every single day—*especially* not when you are exercising it. The purpose of vocal exercising isn't only to improve the voice; it's also to get an idea about which part of the voice may need the most work that day. Once you've discovered your daily vocal problems, you can work on those problem areas by using the suggested exercises in this book. By the time you perform, your entire throat will be operating properly. With the exercises, it will always be a battle as you strive for perfection.

In that sense, many singers grow to enjoy the exercises because of the challenges they face with their voices. You will constantly challenge the voice to perform better. The events of any given day will dictate what that day's challenges will be, what to work on most, what weak areas need exercising, and what good habits to reinforce.

Sometimes a singer will choose not to sing songs for a while and only exercise. It's hard to say whether this is a good idea. Some are overwhelmingly surprised at how much better their voice has gotten once they start singing songs again. On the other hand, the exercises alone are so much work that, if you don't sing songs for a while, you might start thinking that you *can't* sing anymore because the exercises are so hard!

This is not the truth and will *never* be the truth. The more you exercise and strive for perfection, the better your singing voice will get. To test this theory, we suggest you pick a song that was difficult to sing several weeks before you started using this technique and try singing it again. You may be pleasantly surprised.

Exercising and working the voice the way we suggest you work it is only going to keep improving your singing voice, even when you can hear and feel things in the exercises that still don't sound or feel right. The more you *try* to correct something through exercise and thought, the more your brain absorbs what needs to happen inside the throat for you to sing well. Then, when you sing songs, your voice will go to places in the song that you've been training it to go to without having to think about it. The repetitiveness of the exercises, and your willingness to continue challenging yourself by practicing them, is what makes this happen.

So please try to keep in mind that the exercises will always be hard, but singing will not. Also, the following exercises aren't just good for developing the voice and straightening out the rough spots, they are good for warming up before a gig, and warming down after the gig.

Don't get discouraged if you are having trouble with the exercises. We have been doing these exercises for fifteen years and sometimes they are *still* hard, but singing isn't. In fact, singing is a very enjoyable experience today—and that is what we both want for all of you.

The Art of Practicing

Before we move into the exercises for middle voice and placement, it's very important to understand *how* to practice, because it is only through relentless determination and continued work on mind control that you will achieve the desired results.

Trying Is Practice

Few people realize that the act of "trying" is practice. The more you aspire to feel things the right way, the less your voice will be able to fight it. You may get frustrated because old habits may keep your voice from obeying you because of bad habit sense memory. That frustration is a normal part of the process. What matters most is that you don't give up—no matter what. Go back to *trying* to stop whatever bad habit(s) you've acquired, and continue *trying* to direct, sense, and feel your sound in all the "right" places.

Eventually, you will be able to sing correctly 50 percent of the time and incorrectly 50 per cent of the time. But this is a *good* thing because, by this time, you will always know when you are doing it wrong. You will *feel* it. You may not be able to correct it immediately, but with practice, you will also begin to realize what you are doing when you are singing correctly. Once this happens, you can instruct your voice into proper placement. The good news is that, once you've reached this 50-50 mark, it's only a matter of time before you cross over to the other side and your singing is right more often than it's wrong.

Never Assume

It usually takes a couple of weeks to realize how poor techniques can make it much more difficult to sing. Sometimes the singer will feel "right" a few times in the first week of retraining. But getting it right a few times doesn't mean you have it. A good rule of thumb is to *never assume* you have it; the moment you assume you have it is the moment those bad habits start creeping back in. If you haven't been singing correctly for a long time, you can't expect your voice to find the correct placement in just a few hours of practice, or even a few days. Depending on the voice and what kinds of problems you have, this process could take months, or even years. (That may sound discouraging to some of you, but if you *really* want your voice, it's the truth.)

When starting out, try to bear in mind that the "wrong way" is embedded in your sense memory, and that the "right way" must become the *only* way you know how to sing. You must become your own teacher. Learn to detach from your voice and *stop listening* to it. If you are truly concentrating on talking to your voice and giving your voice the proper guidance, there won't be any room for listening to how it sounds. If there is, then you are *not* concentrating.

Use a Recording Device

Your voice must become the student and you must become the guide. To do this, you will have to use a tape recorder or other recording device—preferably one you can keep rewinding after every exercise attempt so you can listen for whether it was wrong or right (*not* for whether it sounded good or bad). Good or bad will keep you judging in a negative way, but right or wrong will keep you evaluating from the teacher's point of view. This is what it means to be listening from a higher perspective.

Things you should listen for are:

- Did you stay on the vowel throughout the exercise and on every single key, or did it change to another vowel or non-vowel sound?

- Is your tongue pulling back or down and/or lying too flat, causing you to feel as if your voice is either trapped or sounding too nasal?

- Are your swallowing muscles tensing and pushing out?

- Are you pinching the sound by squeezing the cords together with your neck muscles to get more of an edge to your sound?

- Are you pushing to get the sound out, and straining with your stomach muscles—getting louder and louder as you try to reach higher and higher notes?

Working in this way—by listening back to yourself on tape—will help you to focus more attention on breaking your bad habits, and less attention on the sound. Nine times out of ten, the reason a voice is not going to the right places (and not bridging) is because there are bad habits in the way. It's these bad habits that are keeping you from having what you want. And without taping, it's easy to fool yourself. Sometimes things won't feel right but you'll rationalize that you are "getting it" because of the way you *think* it sounded, rather than the way it felt. With regard to bridging, middle voice, and placement, you will have to rely on the recording you hear, feeling, and sensation—not how it sounds when you are practicing without recording it.

Our best advice is to invest in a good tape recorder, because the truth will always reveal itself on tape. The tape recorder will become your greatest tool as you forge onward with this work.

Working on Vowels with Your Recording Device

When working on a vowel, it's important to remember that, if the vowel is shaped correctly, then the cords and muscle groups will automatically go into the correct physiological position. Knowing this means that the vowel can't lose shape anywhere in the exercise or on any key of that exercise.

For example, while using the vowel AH on a five-note exercise (12345), you may begin on the AH, but by the time you get to the fifth note, it may have changed to UH. Sometimes you may even *think* you stayed on the vowel, only to play it back on tape and discover that you did not. (This is why taping is the only method by which you can measure your success.) If the vowel changes shape, then the placement also changes. UH will put the voice under the chin, and you will be able to hear when that happens on the tape. If you can't hear it by listening to the tape, try imitating what you just heard aloud. Imitating involves exaggeration, and the exaggeration of the sound you just heard will help you to identify what the problem is. Sometimes you *feel* something go wrong while recording, but can't diagnose it until you listen back and imitate.

If it's not right, then, after imitating what you've heard yourself sing on tape and diagnosing the problem, start over again on that same exercise. This time, try even harder, and use your mind to keep telling yourself to stay true to the vowel. Think *only* about staying true to the vowel and you will subsequently do that very thing. There will be no room for listening to whether you sound good or bad, or wondering if you are using your stomach muscles too much or if your tongue is in the way. Concentrate single-mindedly on telling your voice to stay on that vowel for every pitch. Don't move to another key until you are satisfied that you have done this successfully, that it sounds right, and that it felt free while you were taping it. You'll only know for sure when you listen back.

This, in and of itself, can become a very frustrating experience, and you may not realize how competitive you are until you start practicing like this. You'll be in competition with the tape, your voice, and what you keep hearing when it's wrong. This is when you will know you have detached from the idea that this is *your voice* or that it must *sound* good. Instead, you'll feel and hear what needs correction rather than judging the sound as either good or bad. This makes it easier to become the teacher and will hopefully inspire you to keep going until each problem is corrected. *This* is what the act of *trying* means, and *this* is what the *art* of practice is.

Vowel Exercise

As an exercise, start in any key and sing a five-note (12345) AH, EE, OH, or OO scale into your recorder see if you were able to stay true to your vowel. If there is any pitch on which the vowel lost its shape, you cannot allow yourself to move to the next key until you have successfully stayed on the vowel on all five notes. From time to time you will notice that, each time you tape it, a problem occurs on a different note or set of notes. This process might take a lot more concentration than you first think!

Practicing like this is great for your *entire* voice because, if you concentrate enough to stay true to the vowel in one key on every single pitch, you are likely to be able to do it on the next set. As you move from one register to the next, you may notice that your voice is finally opening up.

Work on Squeezing, Straining, and Pushing with Your Recording Device

Another thing to listen for is whether you can hear squeezing and straining of the neck muscles, or pushing in or up with the stomach muscles. If it sounds pinched, you are using your neck muscles. If it sounds (and feels) like the pitch is hard to reach and you are having to get louder and louder the higher you go, then you are probably straining with the neck and pushing up the stomach muscles to hit the note—maybe even holding your breath for a split second before starting, which forces you to blast air through the vocal cords for sound to come out. If you discover any of these problems, go back and concentrate on removing these obstacles, and keep taping so you can listen for success.

You will know it's right if it was easy and you have air left when you reach the end of an exercise. You'll also know it's right if you were able to keep each pitch at the same level of loudness without breaking. Play back the recording to see if you were right. If it is as you thought, the cords controlled the flow of air and not your body. If you do not have any air left at the end of the exercise, it means the cords were not able to control the flow, and you most likely resorted to controlling it with your stomach and neck muscles rather than just with the diaphragm alone.

If you hear that the sound is trapped somewhere in the back of your throat—much like a squawking bird, or as if you are choking on it—it means that your tongue and/or swallowing muscles under the chin have interfered. Once again, start paying attention to your tongue, keeping it forward in one of the two tongue positions while practicing (also make sure it isn't lying too flat). Keep your fingers on the muscles under the chin to make sure those muscles aren't tightening in any way—that they are staying relaxed as you do your exercises. (Again, if you are not sure what it feels like to have those muscles interfere, put your finger under your chin and swallow. When you do this, you will feel the swallowing muscles tense and pull out. This should not be happening when singing anything unless you are consciously doing it for some sort of effect.)

Bridging the Middle

Breaks usually occur in the mid-to-upper middle range. If you have a break, you have probably noticed that, after the chest voice has reached its limit, the first couple of notes preceding the break might feel and sound weak. You may also notice that the higher you go in the head voice, the stronger that head voice seems to get.

Women and Men Break in the Same Place

The middle register starts for both men and women around middle C (which we refer to as C1). When working on bridging breaks, it's interesting to note that most men and women have breaks in the exact same area. (If your voice hasn't been bridged, you may even have two breaks.) Technically, men and women are supposed to be an octave apart, but when it comes to the breaks, we land in the same areas because men start going into the *upper part of their middle* range when they hit C1, and women start going into the *lower part of their middle* range when they hit C1. This is where each voice type breaks:

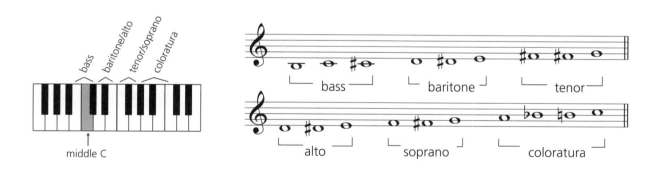

A lot of men habitually push their chest registers up to the top of their upper-middle range. This means they break at about A1 or B1 and can sometimes hit a C2, but all three of these notes will usually feel and sound strained, distorted, or uncontrollable. Likewise, a lot of women have learned to do the same thing and can usually push their chest voice up to C2 without problem, but once they get to C♯2 or D2, it either flips or feels too strained to continue.

Some men and women never learn how to push their chest registers that high. For those men and women, breaks will occur around D1, D♯1, E1, F1, F♯1, or G1. And some singers actually have two discernable breaks that occur in the lower *and* upper part of the middle range. Failed attempts to mask the break by squeezing or pushing with the neck and stomach muscles can cause this to happen.

Breaks Are Caused by Weak Muscle Groups

If you are breaking, then one or both of your muscle groups is weak. As stated earlier, some singers break because they try to push their chest voice too high—until it can't go any further. This is usually such an uncomfortable feeling that, at some point, the voice may be forced to break, just to relieve the pressure.

Remember: to bridge the voice, the arytenoids (at the back of the throat) do most of the stretching, while the thyroid group (at the front) holds in a V-grip position. Technically, the thyroid group acts as bracing tension for the arytenoids as they stretch back for each pitch. The problem we teachers find when trying to bridge a student's voice is this: most singers are unaware that their arytenoids must stretch from the start of their lowest pitches, and that they must continue to stretch for each successively higher pitch. Otherwise, you are only using the chest voice (or thyroid group) alone to try to get through the upper middle register. This usually makes singers resort to manipulating their neck and stomach muscles, or body in some way to get through that section without sounding like they have a break. Forcing your voice to do things this way will not come without its consequences.

Here's a scenario: You're singing a song in mostly chest voice range, and you're really into it except suddenly you become aware that *that* note is coming up. You know: the one you can't sing very well in your chest voice and have a hard time hitting? So you have to leave the emotional content of the song to figure out, in one split second of time, how you are going to hit that note.

Once you get to the note, if it was wrong, everyone knows it was wrong. And if it was right, you'll usually spend the remainder of the song surveying the audience to assess whether that note was good or not. By the time you've finished the song, you're thinking, "That was terrible." You think it was terrible because you had to leave the song to figure out how to approach that note and still have it sound as strong as the rest of your voice. The problem with this method is that you can't gauge how well that note will come out or even if it will be on pitch. You don't have the control over it that you are looking for, and you take the risk of singing flat or sharp every time you go after notes this way.

Start Lightly and Feel the Resonance

When training to bridge the middle, it's best to start with a lighter sound rather than a heavier sound. At this stage in the training, it's more about placement and feeling the cords than it is about the sound.

When singers approach things this way for the first time, they often think their voice sounds weak or wimpy. It's important to remember that this isn't how you will sound when singing songs. This is about *exercising* the muscle groups that control the cords. To do this, you must pretend that the sound is originating on and around the soft palate/oral pharynx area and then heading straight into the mask (cheeks and nose, but not *in* the nose—it must be felt resonating behind the nose). It's a lot harder to feel things in the mask when you blast your voice up from your stomach area. "Mask singing" is just resonance felt in your face; the sound must begin as if it came from the back of your head (on that back wall of the throat directly inside your mouth), rather than from down in the stomach. If it comes from the stomach, you will feel your stomach punch in, or tense up, and subsequently push up the diaphragm just to hit the notes.

When it's done correctly, your diaphragm will automatically expand out. You won't have to tense it to keep it out because the cords will control and compress the air for you. Feeling things in the mouth, cheeks, behind the nose, and up towards the forehead is nearly impossible if you go after sound with the reach of your air and the sheer brute strength of your stomach muscles.

Singing in the Mask and Bridging

The phrase *singing in the mask* refers to sound resonating as it *reaches* the front of the face. It's not felt as intense pressure; it's more like sound and air together (resonance) that is felt traveling higher on a line (like the voice is traveling on a wire), the higher up the head you get.

On the lowest notes, you feel resonance as it reaches its end point (top note) on the hard palate and, depending on the note, you feel it right behind the nose (but not inside of it). To get this feeling, don't squeeze or blow the air up from the stomach, and don't try to pull or push the sound into the front of your face just because you know it's supposed to land there. Again, this has to be done by talking to your voice internally and not with your body.

When you start working with the mask sensation, the feeling is slight and light. It's not supposed to be a powerful, pressurized sensation behind the nose and sinus area. When you apply a lot of pressure, all you really feel is the air pressure and the voice usually doesn't feel (or sound) like it's free. When it's right, some people find themselves asking, "Is this really it?"

If you are learning how to sing in the mask, then you are also learning how to bridge and blend. This placement, in the mask, is what also helps to bridge and blend the voice because the face (like the thyroid group) also acts as bracing tension for the arytenoid group. The face/mask and thyroid group (front of throat muscles and cartilages) will help hold the stretch of the cord as the muscles and cartilages of the arytenoids stretch back and come together for each successively higher note.

Visualize the Sound Moving on a Line

When you exercise your voice, remember to visualize the sound moving on a line (or wire) from the very back of your throat (or head) to the front of your face. The air and sound travels straight along this line when descending (and ascending). Thinking this way will help you keep the cords stretching from front to back in the low register.

If you imagine every descending note moving vertically downward, you may end up placing your notes below your chin, and you may change the shape of your vowel sound! Likewise, as you ascend, you shouldn't think of each note moving higher vertically. This could cause you to squeeze or tighten your cords and neck muscles to reach those higher notes. So always remember to visualize the notes moving on that line from back to front and front to back.

On the low notes, this imagined straight line starts on the back wall of your throat (inside your mouth) and points straight toward the front of your mouth (or hard palate) and keeps travelling beyond it. The highest of those low notes will land on the hard palate (front of the mouth). You will feel middle notes starting a bit higher up— on that wall in the oral pharynx—and it will feel like the straight line of sound heads directly into the cheeks and nose area (not inside the nose, but just behind it). You will feel the highest notes originating at the back of the head (behind the eyes) and heading straight out to, and through, the top of your sinus area.

General Sensation Groupings for Men and Women

In general, the feelings and sensations for mask singing and bridging the voice can be grouped like this:

MEN

- From C-1 to G-1: the notes are primarily felt on the hard palate and heading just above it in the pocket behind the nose.

- From G-1 to D1: the notes will be felt from just above the hard palate and behind the nose as it also begins to enter the lower part of the cheek/sinus area.

- From D1 to A1: the notes will be felt moving upward to the middle of, and behind, the cheek/sinus/nose area.

- From A1 to C2: the notes will be felt as moving from the cheek/sinus area to up behind the bridge of the nose, behind the eyes.

- Anything above the C2 will be felt as going from behind the top of the bridge of the nose and heading out toward the front of the forehead. The higher you go, the higher up in the head you will feel it.

WOMEN

- From G-1 to D1: the notes are primarily felt on the hard palate and heading just above it in the pocket behind the nose.

- From D1 to A1: the notes will be felt as starting from the pocket just above the hard palate and heading up behind the nose and into the sinus/cheek area.

- From A1 to E2: the notes will be felt from the sinus/cheek area and heading up toward, and behind, the bridge of the nose, directly behind the eyes.

- From C2 to G2: the notes will be felt as originating from the back of the head (behind the bridge of the nose and may even be felt as shooting toward the front of the forehead). The higher you go, the higher up in the head you will feel it.

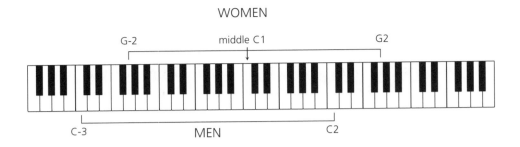

Special note: You can always take *any* of the exercises in this book lower or higher in pitches than what we are working with in the text or on CD. You may want to do this to stretch the muscle groups of the voice as far as you can. But if you do, make sure you're not squeezing, pushing, or straining in any way to do so.)

Exercise: Getting into the Mask and Bridging (123454321)

Men start on C and women start on G, using the vowel AH. The pop/rock AH differs from the classical AH in that it's not as round and vertical in shape and sound. (For example, a classical AH would sound more like the AH in the word "father." For pop, it sounds more like the AH in the word "my," with the AH pronounced slightly more horizontal.) The pop/rock AH is considerably more forward on the hard palate and in the mask. You will also feel the resonance as more horizontal than vertical (as it is in classical singing).

On the first note, you should feel the resonance (meaning the air and the sound together) on both the soft palate and near the back of the hard palate. Try to imagine that *this* is your originating point, and that the starting point is *not* down inside your neck where the cords are literally located. Instead, imagine your cords as if the backs of them (the arytenoids) begin in the hole at the back wall of the tube in your throat.

As you travel from note to note in the exercise, you should notice that the resonance starts to lean (but isn't pushed or pulled from your stomach muscles) more toward the front of the face. If you are doing it right, you might feel the resonance take some kind of form or shape inside your mouth. (Some singers describe it as a "potato" sitting in their mouth.) If you don't feel anything, just keep working at it until you do. Sometimes it takes a while to move away from listening to the sound of your voice and getting into feeling it. (If you are one of these types of people, it will take a great deal of concentration on your part to keep telling your voice what it is supposed to be doing and where it is supposed to feel like it starts and ends, while also telling it to stay true to the vowel.)

The more you try to imagine and visualize it, the more you may begin to sense and feel that this is how it *does* feel when it's done correctly (even if we know that physiologically it happens differently and that you're instructed to only imagine it this way for placement and sensation). Again, there is nothing you can do to physically make these things happen, short of sticking your fingers down your throat and using them to pull back on the cords and make them stretch! Every bit of this is done with the power of your mind, thought, concentration, and visualization.

If you keep visualizing, you will eventually feel these things we've described. You will also start feeling when you've done it wrong. Remember this: *you can't do it right until you have done it wrong, and you can't do it well until you have done it badly.*

Before you actually start performing this exercise, it's important to note that the first note of each key should not begin with a lot of power or tightness or a heavy chest sound. The whole idea of this exercise is to get a feel for what it's like to be singing in the mask. If you begin too heavily (which means you may be starting too deep in the throat) you will have to start getting louder by the time you get to the fifth note. Getting louder as you ascend usually means that you are pushing your stomach muscles up, which pushes up the diaphragm, squeezes the neck, and forces you to BLOW your air out. Each note must remain at the exact same volume you started with. Remember: we are trying to find a level of loudness that you can work at without breaking. If that means that you have to start in a voice that feels and sounds similar to your head voice, then that's where you have to begin. Otherwise, you'll only be reinforcing bad habits.

For men the range we're working with is from C-1 to C2. For women it's G-1 to G2. This is a two-octave range for both men and women. The reason we work these two specific octaves in both the male and female voice is because they cover the entire middle range of both voices from low to high. Technically, if you can sing the highest note in exercise well, then approximately four notes below that top note will be sung well in a song. The reverse is true for the lowest note. The idea behind this is that the farther you are able to stretch the cords from front to back, from the lowest to the highest notes without breaking, then the stronger the middle range will be when you actually start singing songs.

Mask and Bridging Exercise for Men

To begin, men should feel the first note of each key from C-1 to G-1 originating in the oral pharynx/soft palate/back of hard palate area. Picture that *that* first note starts there, as if the cords and sound are located there (even though they aren't). On the highest note of this group (the 5th), with each successive degree, the resonance should feel like it's moving farther up front on the hard palate, right behind the front teeth. Once your lowest note begins at G-1, the first note of each new key from G-1 to C1 should also be felt in the same places. The resonance of the highest of those notes (the 5th) should then be felt at the front of the hard palate (and moving towards the pocket just above it).

From C1 to G1, the first note of each new key should feel as if it is starting on the middle of the hard palate. The highest notes' resonance will then feel like it's moving more *behind* the nose and nasal cavity. Do not try to push the sound into the nose tofeel it in the nasal cavity. It's a better idea to think of it *behind* the nasal cavity, to avoid straining and sounding too nasal.

From G1 to C2, the first note of each new key should feel as if it is starting on the front of the hard palate (behind the teeth), and the highest notes' resonance should feel as though it's moving more toward the bridge of the nose (just behind the eyes).

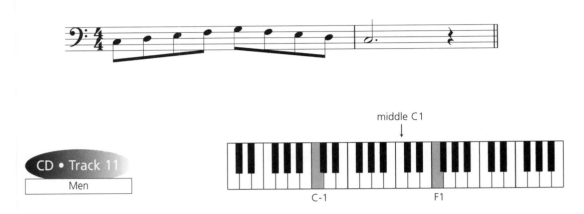

Mask and Bridging Exercise for Women

For the women: You should feel the first note of each key from G-1 to C1 as starting on and around the oral pharynx/ soft palate/back of hard palate area. You have to picture it enough to actually be able to start feeling it there. On the highest notes of this group (the 5th), the resonance should feel as though it's moving more toward the front of the mouth on the hard palate (right behind the teeth.)

Once it gets to C1, the first note of each new key from C1 to G1 should feel as if it is starting, once again, right behind the upper front teeth on the hard palate. On the highest notes (the 5), the resonance should feel like it moves further toward the front of the hard palate with each successive degree (and/or moving forward into the pocket just above it).

From G1 to C2, the first note of each new key should feel as if it is starting on the middle of the hard palate. On the highest notes (the 5), the resonance should feel like it moves more behind the nose and into the nasal cavity (cheeks). Again, do not squeeze or push the sound up and into the nasal cavity (your cheeks) in your attempt to feel it there by using the abdominal muscles. It's best to *picture* and not push or pull the sound into those cavities with those muscles in any way (to avoid strain and sounding too nasal) as the resonance comes up just behind the nasal cavity.

From C2 to G2, the first note of each new key should feel like it is starting at the front of the hard palate, and on the highest notes (the 5), the resonance should feel more like it comes up behind the bridge of the nose (behind the eyes) with each successive note.

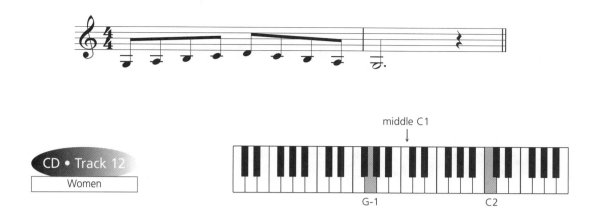

Exercise: Changing the Vowel (123454321)

When you are changing the vowels, each vowel must stay with the same placement as the one you just worked on. Why? Because it helps with bridging, blending, and resonance.

One way to learn how to change the vowel, for example, is to start on a vowel like AH and then change that vowel to EE. Use AH to ascend on the first part of the exercise (12345), hold out the AH on the 5, and while you hold out the AH, change it to EE all in one breath (while keeping the exact same placement you had on that AH). This means you can't change your lips or jaw much at all.

Remember that vowel formation takes place around the oral pharynx and soft palate area. That area is like a big hole inside your mouth and at the back of your throat (in between your ears). Go all the way through the entire exercise working it this way, 12345, changing from AH to EE on the 5. If the sound is properly placed, you will not only feel the AH and EE as it shapes around the soft palate/oral pharynx area, but you should feel the resonance (air and sound) moving across the palate from the soft to the hard from note to note. This is what the term *more forward* really means.

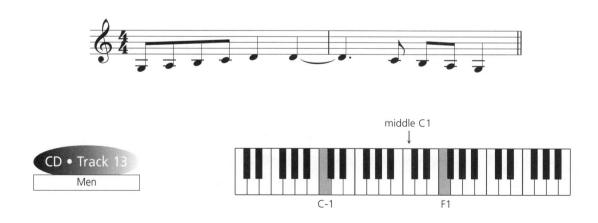

CD • Track 14
Women

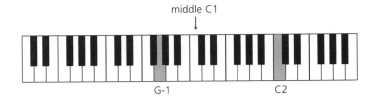

middle C1

G-1

C2

Once you successfully change to the EE on the 5, try changing the exercise by adding the descent from the 5 (54321), staying on the EE. This means the first 5 notes will be AH (12345) and on the 5th note you will change the vowel from AH to EE (still on one breath) and then descend on EE (54321).

After you have successfully gone through this exercise on AH/EE, try the entire exercise (123454321) on EE alone. (Remember, men are working from C-1 to C2, and women are working from G-1 to G2.)

To get placement on other vowels, use this same technique, but try it with a new vowel of your choice. (Tip: Some singers find switching from EE to EH, OO to OH, and AH to OH or vice versa easier than switching with other combinations, but it's best to try as many combinations as possible so that you get good at all of them.)

Something to Think About: Pushing and Squeezing

All your notes should be clear in tone. You shouldn't hear any escaping air with or without the tape. If you do hear escaping air, it means that you may be blowing your air through the cords, or that you are squeezing and then trying to push your air through the cords to get the sound out.

Blowing is different from squeezing in that there just isn't enough cord effort, and the sound will end up with more air than edge. Blowing means the cords are open too wide (from side to side). On the contrary, if you are squeezing, the cords are too close together (tight), and this will force you to push the air through to get the sound out because no sound can come out unless air passes by the cords.

To get a feel for tightness, just squeeze in your stomach muscles and try whispering. When you whisper, you can actually feel the cords tighten to make the sound. Unless you are literally blowing air through the cords to try to whisper—which is very hard to do—whispering makes the cords rub together. It's this kind of tightening that is also known as squeezing. It means the cords are too closed (from front to back). (As a side note, *never whisper*, even when you are sick. If you are sick and have laryngitis or can't speak, write notes to communicate. Whispering too much can actually cause hoarseness or make whatever condition you have, like laryngitis, even worse.)

Most singers try to get a more edgy sound for the pop, rock, and R&B voice by slamming their cords shut and by using the stomach and neck muscles to squeeze the cords together. Singers literally close the entire mechanism to achieve these styles and types of sound when, in truth, only the back end of the cords (the arytenoids) should be coming together and stretching further backwards the higher you go. Again, there must always be a slight amount of air passing through the cords for correct sound, and that cannot happen if the entire mechanism is slammed shut by your stomach and neck pinching inwards.

The arytenoids, when you are singing correctly, will work very hard to stay together in the back and to stretch backwards the higher you go. But, you should not tighten with your neck muscles or inside your throat (with the cords) to try to achieve this. Again, approaching things in this way will only make it so that no air can pass through, and it forces you to push the air up from your stomach to get the sound out (this will cause the diaphragm to punch up and inwards, preventing it from expanding outwardly to create the support needed for the cords). Instead, by pushing up air like this, your diaphragm collapses when it jumps inwardly, leaving you with no support for the mechanism.

An edgy pop/rock sound is tricky, and can be dangerous if you don't know what you are doing. You can sound great to yourself and others when you manipulate your sound (and body) in unnatural ways to achieve a style, but you also may be doing damage at the same time (if you are not educated about the right and wrong ways.)

If you feel strain in any way, soreness in any part of your throat, then it is wrong, and you are probably squeezing and pushing. Habits like this are very hard to break but they *must* be broken. The *only* way you can break bad habits is by repeatedly thinking and talking to your voice about the right thing to do, stopping yourself when you know it's wrong, concentrating, and continuing to exercise the two vocal cord groups. Only then will you become familiar enough with the right way.

More Bridging and Mask Exercises

Blending Exercise (13531)

This next exercise starts with the vowel EE. Again, men start at C-1 and women start at G-1. The first note for both males and females should feel like it is originating from and around the oral pharynx/soft palate/back of hard palate area. This means you should try to *feel* the sound and air starting *together* (at the exact same moment in that spot), and as you proceed, you should then feel the column of air and sound move toward the front of your face on each successive note, as if it were riding along a wire in that direction.

We urge you to picture the sound as if it starts in the oral pharynx, even though the vocal cords are anatomically located inside the neck. Don't try to push the air from the stomach or squeeze the sound with your neck muscles to get it to go towards the front of the face. Use the face as bracing tension for the arytenoids, just as you use the thyroid group at the front of the throat for bracing tension as the cords stretch backwards to create each new pitch. When it is done right, the resonance feels as if it is *pointing* right behind the nose.

The Vowel EE

Many people have trouble with the vowel EE because they have a tendency to clamp their jaw shut and tighten the cords to pronounce it. (Refer to the mouth illustrations in chapter 3 if you need to see mouth positions again.)

The way to correctly pronounce the EE is to think of it being pronounced at the top of the tube/pharynx and traveling further forward on each successively higher note as it makes its way across the hard palate, until it reaches the top note right behind the upper front teeth. When you picture this, you may start to *feel* the sound not only coming up from the top of the tube, but you may feel as if it *has* started on and around the oral pharynx. As you ascend, you should feel the air moving more forward on the hard palate.

Men should feel the sensation start to move up behind the space between their upper lip and nose by the time they hit the G-1 on the 5; for women, it should start by the time they hit the D1 on the 5.

As the men move into the midsection of their middle range (around C1), the first note will feel like it begins on the hard palate. As you ascend to the 3 and 5, you should feel the air moving slightly more forward (almost behind the nose) on the hard palate with each one of those notes.

For women, these same sensations will start on D1. As you ascend to the 3 and the 5, you should feel the air move slightly more forward (almost behind the nose) on the hard palate with each one of those notes.

For both men and women: as you ascend on 135, try to sense-memorize what you are doing so that you can duplicate these sensations on the way back down (531). Often, singers will do fine going up the scale (135), but as soon as they begin to descend (531), their voice starts losing the placement and falling below the mouth level. The vowel may have even changed shape. (For example, it may change from EE to IH, as in the word "this." Sometimes it even changes to OO, as in the word "shoe".)If the vowel changes shape, it could mean that the cords have lost their stretch in the back; this is what makes the tone sound as if it has fallen under the chin. You may also have even invited those "under the chin" muscles in your attempts to hit the lower notes.

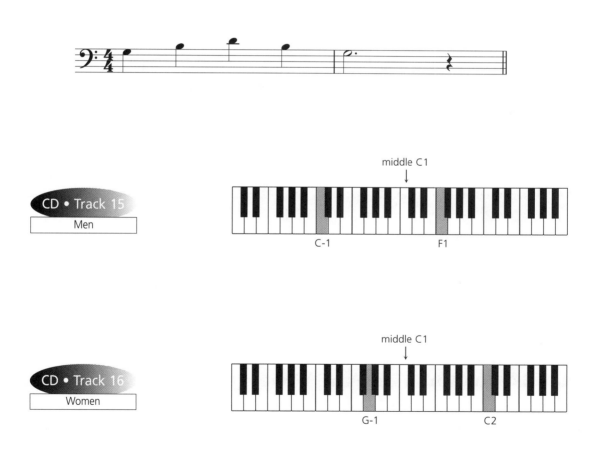

The Secret to Blending

The whole idea behind bridging and blending is to keep *everything* "in the mask" from the mouth area to the forehead. If you are dipping below mouth area on the lower notes, no matter how low they are, you are not in the mask—your cords are losing stretch, and other muscle groups under the chin, neck, or stomach are trying to help you.

A good rule of thumb is to try to make sure that all your starting notes feel as though they originate around the oral pharynx, but as you proceed, the notes should feel as if they are moving more toward the front of the hard palate. The higher you go, you should start feeling the resonance as it comes up behind your nose, then behind the cheeks, and finally behind the eye area as you get higher up. If the starting notes are not correct, the rest of the exercise won't be correct either. The only way to know for sure is by taping yourself as you do it.

You can even tape as you sing along with the CD. This will at least tell you if you are matching pitch. If your vowel changes shape, you must work the area where you hear this happening (e.g., the 3rd or 4th note, either up or down) until you hear that vowel staying true to itself on your tape.

By the time you reach the upper end of the middle range (for men this is anywhere from F1 to C2, and for women this is anywhere from A1 to G2), your starting note (the 1) should feel as if it originates on the front of the hard palate—just above the pocket there. You should feel the 3 just behind the nose, and then into the sinus/cheek area. You should feel the 5 right up, and behind, the bridge of the nose, but you should not squeeze or push by using the abdominal cavities to get the sound to go there. If men decide to go even higher than C2, then those notes should be felt more vertically, just above the bridge of the nose (beginning of forehead). The same holds true for women when reaching G2 and anything above this note.

Remember that the higher you go, the higher you'll feel the sound in your head. Again, try to sense-memorize your placement, and if you are not sure if you are getting it, tape yourself.

Exercise for Changing the Vowels (13531)

Now that you have mastered EE, let's work on changing the vowel, while keeping the same placement we had on EE. This time, after you ascend on EE (135), change the vowel from EE to OO (as in the word "ewe") all in one breath—while you are on the 5. Hold out the EE just a bit before changing to OO, so you can feel that placement, and then descend on OO (531). Listen to the example on the CD. You should experience all the same sensations as you did when working on EE. Once you have completed the entire exercise like this, do it again but all on OO (13531).

Here, we're working with combinations that require the cords to stretch from front to back, and side to side (though none of this can be seen with the naked eye, technically this is what is happening on these vowels). EE stretches the cords from front to back, while OO (an air vowel) pulls them apart (from side to side).

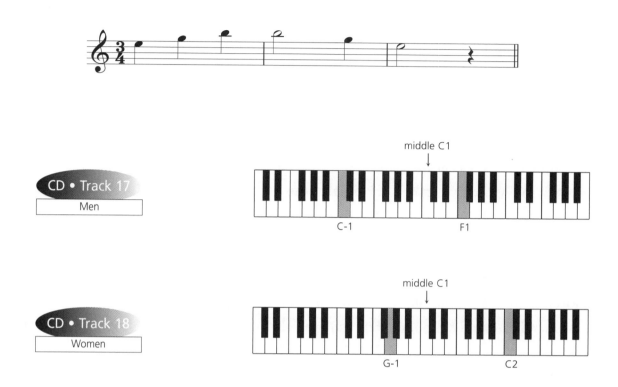

Repeat This Exercise Using AH

Now try the 13531 exercise using the vowel AH (as in the word "my"; this is the pop/rock AH). AH also stretches the cords from front to back, just not as much as EE.

As already mentioned, many singers have trouble with the pop/rock AH because it can't be a classical AH (as in the word 'father'). When starting this AH, it won't sound like AH at all from inside your head. That's because this AH has to land so far forward in your face on that first note that it almost sounds whiney, or modified with an AW (like that of a bird caw-ing). Be sure to tape yourself while performing this exercise.

When you do it correctly, you may be surprised that it *does* sound like an AH on tape, after knowing it didn't sound like that inside your head. If you are doing it wrong, when you play back the tape, you may hear the AH trapped in the back of your throat (instead of forward). If this happens, your tongue may be laying too flat. It is very important—especially on this vowel—that you try to feel the air of that first note as far forward on the hard palate as you possibly can, without squeezing or pushing the sound into the nose, or closing the nasal passages. (It has to fall just behind the nose, not in it.)

Again, men will start at C-1 and women at G-1. As you ascend, you should feel the vowel staying on the hard palate. Once the 5 hits C1 for men and D1 for women, you should start feeling those notes move just above the hard palate, and in the pocket behind the nose. The higher you go, the more notes you will feel in the cheek or sinus area, especially as men reach F1 and women reach A1.

When the men hit A1, B1, and C2, the air from the AH should be felt up behind, and slightly above, the bridge of the nose (behind the eyes); any higher than that, and it will be felt in the forehead. The same is true for women once you hit C2, C#2, D2, or D#2. Any higher than that and those notes, like the men, will be felt in the forehead.

Repeat This Exercise with OH

Once you successfully complete this exercise all on AH, do it again, but this time change the AH to OH on the 5. Hold out the AH for a moment before changing to OH, so you can maintain the placement as you make the switch. Make sure the OH is in the same placement as the AH and that you truly feel it in that placement. OH, like OO, is also an air vowel, so it technically pulls the cords apart (stretches them from side to side) while AH stretches the cords from front to back (pulling them in and more together). While this is what happens, none of it can be seen with the naked eye.

Once you have changed to the OH (on the 5), descend from 5 to 3 to 1 with it. So, the exercise is AH on 135, change from AH to OH on 5, and OH on 531. All the same feelings and sensations must be felt with these two vowels as they were felt when you performed the exercise solely on AH. After completing the exercise in this way, do the entire exercise on OH alone.

Exercise with the Vowels EH and OH (135354321)

The vowels for this exercise are EH and OH. EH (as in the word "they") is sung on 1353, and OH is sung on 54321. Men start on C-1 and women start on G-1. For both men and women, the air and the sound (vibration of sound and/or resonance) on the first note (the 1) should feel as if it is originating around the oral pharynx (soft palate/back of hard palate area). The top notes (35354) should feel as if they are gradually moving toward the front of the hard palate with each successive note.

With the 3 and 5, the sound should feel as though it is leaning *even more forward* on the hard palate. The 5 will be felt not only on the hard palate, but also in the pocket just above it, right behind the nose. When you get to the 5, you have to sense-memorize the sensation felt on that EH because, when you come back to the 5, you must switch to OH while keeping the exact same placement you had on EH.

Once you begin to descend on the OH (54321), try to keep the sound on the hard palate. Do not allow it to drop under and into the chin or too far down into the throat, or your cords will lose their stretch and your vowel will probably change shape. Make sure your vowel is staying true and not modifying to UH as you descend. You must feel the sound and air staying in the mask (face). Remember to tape, tape, tape!

By the time you get to C1 (men) or D1 (women) on the *first* 5 of this exercise, you should start feeling that note as if it has risen just above the pocket behind the nose. Again, sense-memorize the placement so that when you switch to the OH on the second 5, you feel in the exact same place as you did for the EH.

EH and OH Exercise for Men

For men, as you ascend into the upper-middle register (D1 through G1) on the first 5 of each new key, you should feel these notes moving toward, and coming up behind, the nose and into the sinus and cheek area, with each one resonating a little higher than that of the key just before it. By the time you get to F1, F♯1, or G1 of each new key, you should definitely be feeling these notes behind the nose and in the sinus and cheek area (but don't squeeze or push the sound to get it there) by using the abdominal muscles.

When men finally get into the lower part of their high register (G♯1 through C2) on the 5 of each new key, they should start feeling these notes moving gradually up and behind the bridge of the nose, with each one slightly higher up than the one before it. By the time you get to C2, you may even start feeling it going somewhere between the bridge of the nose and the forehead. If you choose to go higher than C2, just remember that the higher you go, the higher up in the head you should feel those notes, and that it has to be done without squeezing or pushing to try to get it up there.

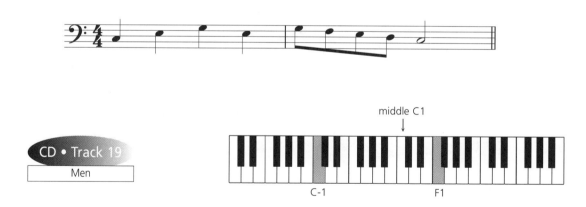

CD • Track 19

Men

middle C1

C-1   F1

EH and OH Exercise for Women

For women, as you ascend from your lower-middle register into your upper-middle register (D1 through F♯1) on the 5 of each new key, you will feel the notes coming up behind the nose and into the sinus or cheek area, with each successive time feeling just a little higher than that of the key before it. By the time you get to F♯1, F1, and G1 (on the 5 of each new key), you should feel those notes right behind the middle of your nose and in the sinus or cheek area (of course, don't squeeze or push the sound to get it there) by using the abdominal muscles. As you ascend to the 5 in each key (from G♯1 to C2), you should start feeling those notes head even further up behind the nose until they finally reach the top of the sinus and bridge of the nose area on the C2.

As you head into the lower part of your high register (C♯2 through G2) on the first 5 of each new key, each one of those high notes should be felt creeping just a little higher up on your face than it was in the key before it. (You should feel them heading up behind the bridge of the nose and into the forehead.) If you choose to go higher than G2, just remember that the higher you go, the higher up in the head you should feel those notes (and remember that it has to be done without squeezing or pushing to get it up there!).

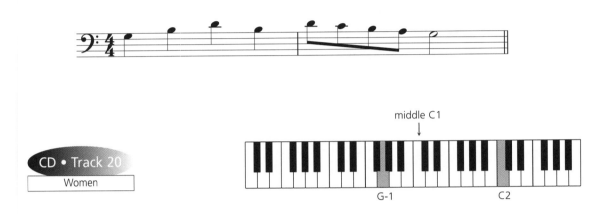

CD • Track 20

Women

middle C1

G-1

C2

Feel free to take all of these exercises and work even lower or higher than just the two octaves, but be sure you don't squeeze, push, or strain in any way. Always remember that the higher you go, the higher up in your head you should feel things and that, no matter how low you go, the resonance should always be felt on the hard palate and never drop below mouth level.

Use of the Slide

Sliding can help the voice move to a note without breaking. When done correctly, it helps with bridging. However, sliding should not be allowed to become a crutch because it can invite pitch problems into your songs.

1–5–1 Exercise

On this exercise, we will again work with two octaves: men from C-1 to C2, and women from G-1 to G2. The idea of this exercise is to slide from the 1 to the 5 and back down to the 1 again without breaking. It's extremely important not to slide too quickly on either the ascent or the descent. The purpose is to keep it connected while also keeping the sound consistent as you slide at the same level of loudness from the bottom to the top, and back down again. If you slide up or down too quickly, you can't keep the stretch at the back of the cords, and we want to make sure that you maintain a good stretch for muscle memory. Once you reach the 5, it's a good idea to hold it out for a second just so you can feel where the note lands and if it feels like it landed in the mask correctly. If it didn't feel that way to you, check your tape to see what might have happened.

Start this exercise using the vowel EH. There is no particular reason for starting with this vowel, except that it is a more open vowel than AH or EE. Yet, just like AH and EE, EH stretches the cords from front to back. We want to work with the vowels that stretch from front to back because we are trying to strengthen the arytenoid group. Eventually, you should be able to move to OH and OO as well, without losing that arytenoid stretch. Just like you did with the other exercises, you should practice this exercise on all the vowels.

When you slide, be especially careful not to squeeze or push the sound into the mask just to get it into the correct spot by using the abdominal muscles. There is a tendency to do that with this exercise, because the sound is so much like a siren that singers may get carried away in their efforts to feel what they've been told they should be feeling as they ascend up and behind the nose and into the sinus, cheek, and forehead area. Do not push it. Try to just feel and sense the sound and air going to those places. The more you try to visualize where the placement should be, the better chance you will have of finally sensing and feeling it there.

For both men and women: when you start the first note, you should feel that note as if it starts around the oral pharynx/soft palate/back of hard palate area. As you slide up to the 5, you should feel the slide (the sound and the air) moving more forward. By the time you reach the 5, you should feel the note just above the upper front teeth on the hard palate. Again, make sure you are not squeezing or pushing the sound to get it there. As you slide back down, try to keep the slide as strong as it was on the way up, and do not allow the sound to drop below mouth level once you have come back to the 1. That last note (the 1) should land in the exact same placement as when you began this exercise on the first note (the 1). (If you are having trouble maintaining the 1 placement, you must keep working on the 1 until you have sense-memorized the placement well enough to slide up to the 5 and come back down to that 1 placement without dropping below mouth level.)

As you keep ascending in each key, the first notes (1) should feel like they move more forward on the hard palate, and the top notes (5) should feel like they move higher in the mask area (behind the nose and in the cheek and sinus area) as you keep ascending. When ascending on the slide, you should also feel the slide itself rising farther up into the mask area. Do not squeeze or push to get it to do that by using the abdominal muscles. And again, on the way back down, be sure your slide does not drop below that mouth area. The 1 should land exactly where you started it at the beginning of the five-note run.

By the time you get to the top (5) notes (for men this is G1 to C2, and for women this is C2 to G2), you should be feeling the 1 as if it starts in the pocket just above the upper front teeth; and as you slide up to the 5, you should feel the slide moving farther and farther up from behind the nose and into the sinus and cheek area until you feel the 5 at the top of the bridge of the nose and forehead area. Again, do not squeeze or push to get the sound to go there by using the abdominal muscles. Also, make sure that, as you slide back down to the 1, it lands in the exact same placement at which you started it.

Once you have ascended to the top of the two-octave ranges, begin your descent in each key until you reach the bottom of the two-octave ranges. (Again, for men, this two-octave range is C-1 to C2 and for women it's G-1 to G2.) All the feelings and sensations felt while ascending this exercise should be felt in all the same areas while descending. Be mindful that the lower you go, the lower you will feel it in the mask. However, all the lowest notes will never drop below the mouth level and hard palate area.

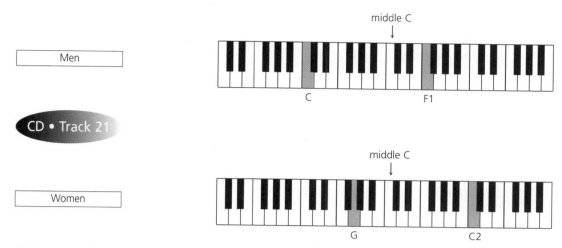

*Women should refer to the men's demonstration on the CD.

1–5, 54321 Exercise

Here we will work with the slide to connect the voice, but this time we will vary it by not sliding on the descent, to see how well you can keep each note connected—without breaking—as you descend note by note.

Men will work from C-1 to C2, and women will work from G-1 to G2. Remember: you can work lower or higher than that if you like, but make sure not to squeeze, push, or strain in any way.

This time, we will start with the vowel OH. Both men and women should feel that first OH as if it originates in the oral pharynx/soft palate/back of hard palate area and finally landing (on the 5) on or near the front of the hard palate. Remember that the OH has the same placement as the AH, so be sure you feel it there. (You may have to perform an AH and then change it to OH so you can be sure of the placement.) *The only difference between these two vowels is lip shaping.* (It is the shape of the lips on OH that give that OH its sound.) You should feel the 5 just behind the upper front teeth on the hard palate.

Try to start at an appropriate volume that will keep the voice from breaking. If you start too heavily in the chest voice, it may start breaking at your breaking points. To ensure that this doesn't happen, you may have to try different volume levels and work up to your break points a few times before finding the volume level that permits you to go through your break smoothly. The idea is to have the voice sound like one voice from the bottom of the range to the top, and back down again.

When you get to the 5 in each new key, hold it out for a second before descending. Again, the reason for holding it is to give you a chance to feel the placement. If you can't feel it, keep doing it until you do. Check to see if you are feeling air where described. If you can feel the air, chances are that you will feel the vibration of the sound in those places as well.

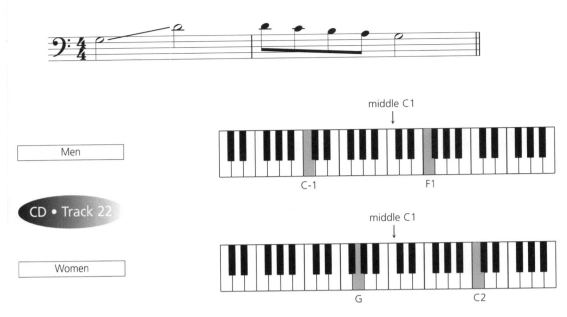

 CD • Track 22

*Women should refer to the men's demonstration on the CD.

Once you have mastered the exercise on OH, change the vowels. In order to properly bridge the voice, you must get the placement right on every vowel, not just one.

Remember: It's All About the Feeling

It's important to get a handle on the feelings, because the face is used as bracing tension and for pressure—not in the stomach. If you can't get a handle on these feelings and sensations, you won't be able to use your face or mask in this way and will resort to pushing the slide (from the 1 to the 5) by using your stomach muscles and air to get it to go where you know you are supposed to be feeling it. Remember: you want your cords to stretch with your ability to visualize *them* doing the work, talking to your voice, and not using your entire body.

You should feel all the lowest notes in this two-octave range as if they start on that hard palate. As you begin to get up to, and through, the middle part of your range, the 5 in each new key should feel as if it's coming up behind the nose and into the sinus and cheek area. The higher you go, the more you should feel it coming up toward the bridge of the nose. The highest notes should be felt behind the bridge of the nose (or right behind the eyes) and even in the forehead (depending on whether you are practicing more than just the two octaves).

Ascend to the top of the two-octave range and then descend back down to the bottom. Descending doesn't mean that your sensations will change. All the same sensations should be felt, only in reverse. Again, this means that as you descend, your highest notes will be felt high in the mask; as you descend, those sensations will fall lower and lower for each consecutive key—but never lower than the mouth or hard palate area, no matter how low you go.

52

1–8, 87654321 Exercise

This exercise is similar to the previous one, except that you now slide through an entire octave before descending note-to-note in the exercise. We'll use the same two octaves we used in the last exercise for both men and women. (Men start at C-1 and go to C2; women start at G-1 and end at G2.)

This time, we will start on the vowel EE. The starting note (1) should feel as if it originates in the middle of the hard palate, while the 8 should feel as if it lands just behind the middle of the nose, and into the cheek and sinus area. Again, hold out the 8 for a second so you can see if you feel the sensation in that area. Once you do, descend note-to-note (87654321) and see if you can stay connected all the way down to the 1. All of those notes should stay between the nose/sinus/cheek area and the hard palate.

By the time men start the scale on C-1 and the women start it on G-1, those notes should feel as though they originate just above the pocket of the hard palate and behind the nose. You should feel the 8 at the top of the bridge of the nose, just behind it. Do not squeeze or push with the diaphragm by using the abdominal muscles as you are going up to the 8. Also, do not get louder as you go higher. This would mean you are pushing to get into the correct placement. Again, remember: it's the stretch of cord and the art of visualization that accomplishes this.

Each note should have the same level of loudness. Once you begin to descend, all of those notes should be felt descending from the top of the bridge of the nose down to the pocket just above the hard palate.

As you descend back into the middle and lower ranges, the lowest notes should be felt on the hard palate, and the higher ones should be felt just behind the nose and in the cheek and sinus area.

Again, make sure to work at a volume level that keeps you from breaking. You might have to play around with those levels until you find one that keeps the voice sounding like one voice throughout the exercise. However, you should notice that, as you ascend, the voice gets a little thinner. But this doesn't mean that it should break or flip registers; thin does not mean airy. There should be good cord stretching, otherwise the sound will be breathy and strained, and it may fall apart.

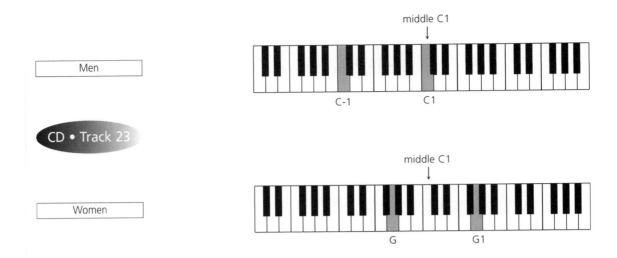

Once you're successful on EE throughout the two octaves, try changing vowels. Again, it's best to master all of the vowels when learning how to bridge.

1358531 Exercise

By this time, you should have a good idea of all the sensations you are supposed to feel on any given note. This is a good exercise for moving from one register to the next because it covers an entire octave, and it also *tests* whether you are able to stay connected as you move from the lowest note to the highest note in the octave.

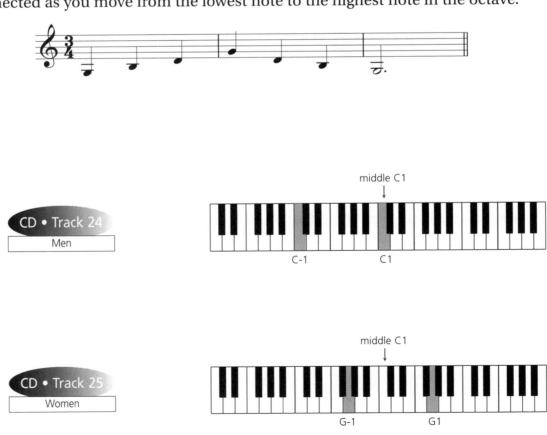

Staying Connected

On the 1, you are at the lowest part of the register, and on the 8, you have reached the highest part of the register. If you are not able to stay connected, take it more slowly. Some singers have a harder time ascending than they do descending, and vice versa. Whichever is the case for you, it is important to work on the area where you felt your voice weaken or break. This may mean working only two notes at a time until it is smooth. If the problem happens while ascending, then, once you have worked the trouble spot enough, try ascending again, all the way to the 8. If it still gives you problems, you must either work the area again, or work another exercise that will help strengthen that particular area.

The reverse is true if the problem takes place while descending. Work the area until it gets stronger and then try descending once again, all the way down to the 1, or use another exercise that will help strengthen that particular area until you feel confident enough to try this exercise again. Start on a vowel of your choosing. Eventually you should go through this exercise on every vowel. Some vowels won't cause a problem, while others might not work as well. All this means is that you need more work on the vowel (or vowels) that gives you trouble. Everyone has at least one troublesome vowel, and everyone is different when it comes to which one.

Once things are smooth and you are staying connected, complete the entire exercise, ascending and descending. Work at least the two-octave minimum. You can go lower or higher if you want; just make sure you are not squeezing, pushing, or straining in any way if you do.

Strengthening the Voice

For a stronger voice, it's important to sense when you can add a little more weight to it without it breaking. If you have been successful with all of the exercises thus far, and can feel the placement, then it's time.

Bear in mind that as your voice gets stronger, you must still have all the feelings and sensations that you did when the voice was lighter, and your larynx must feel very open on the inside. Take your fingers and put them on either side of the larynx to remind yourself of how open that sound must feel.

You should also be feeling the vowel as if the sound originates in the oral pharynx. As you start to add weight to your cords to make the sound heavier (more chest-like), it is especially important to picture the pronunciation and shaping of the vowels as if they start around the soft palate area. As you go higher, imagine the vowels as if they originate above the soft palate area; on the highest notes, you should imagine them higher up in your head (in the back). This entire area is where all your mental picturing must take place. Additionally, the soft palate will feel like it expands from side to side, and the back of your throat (where the tube begins) should feel very open.

Again, the air must come out as if it has started at the back of your head and, with each successive note, moves straight to the front of your face. Do not start from down in the stomach or you will definitely start feeling strain as you try to go higher. Air should come through (between) the vocal cords, but it shouldn't be blasting through there. If that starts happening, then you are squeezing your cords together with your neck muscles or pushing the stomach up and inwards. You must go back to the idea that the vowels should feel like they start their shape in the pharynx—not inside the throat or between the cords.

HEY Exercise (54321)

Men start at G-1 and women start at D1. Using your chest voice, start your first note on the word HEY (as in the word "they") and try to feel that top note originating on the soft palate and heading toward the front of the hard palate, while also making sure that all your lowest notes never drop below the hard palate area. Also, imagine that the air comes from the *back* of your head and moves straight to the front of your face with each successive note.

By the time you get to the middle area of your voice (for men, this will be D1 to F1 or G1; and for women, this will be E1 to G1 or A1), you should start feeling as if the shaping of the word HEY begins *just above* the soft palate area (and making its way toward, and behind, the nose). Make sure you are not squeezing. There has to be air-flow between the cords, but you also want to make sure you are not blasting it through there with your stomach muscles. (The tendency with the "H" is to want to blow it out.) Stay mindful to keep yourself away from the blowing-HUH urge.

As you make your way through the middle area and get to the upper-middle area (for men, this means G1 to D2; for women, this means A1 to E2), start imagining the word shape originating higher up, at the back of the head, above the soft palate and heading toward the bridge of your nose. In that same area, you should also feel as if the air shoots straight from the back of the head to the front of the face on each successive note.

As you get into the highest areas (for men, anything above D2; for women, anything above E2), imagine the sound starting at the back of the head or forehead level and heading towards and behind your eyes and eyebrows (and top of the bridge of the nose area). Again, the air should feel as if it shoots straight from the back of the head to the front of the face on each successive note.

You should not have to switch from chest to head voice at any time while performing this exercise. You must try to keep what will seem a chest-like sound (or full voice) all the way through the exercise. The voice will start thinning as it gets to the mid-to-upper-middle area, and thin even more as it reaches the highest notes, but it should not break. Also, make sure you are not squeezing or pushing to get up into the higher areas. You really have to rely on your ability to picture what has been described. It's the only way you will finally get it.

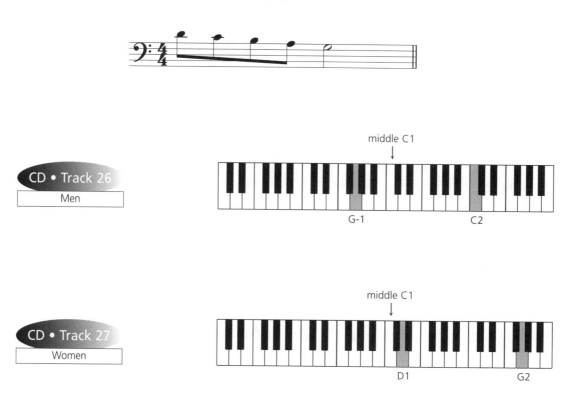

Stay on Your Vowels

Always make sure you stay on your vowel sound. Tape yourself to double-check that you haven't changed it to HEH (as in the word "then"), HAA (as in the word "cat"), or HIH (as in the word "this"). Keeping the EY (as in the word "they") part of the HEY is crucial, because of the open shape this particular vowel sound creates (which is quite open in feel and sound).

HEY Exercise #2 (54321, 123454321)

This exercise requires you to descend on the 54321, followed by an ascent up to 5 and descent back to 1. Make a concerted effort to sense-memorize the placement of the very first note (the 5). Also, continue to make sure that all your lowest notes never drop below the mouth or hard palate area.

As soon as you get down to the 1, start that first note in exactly the same place and try to ascend to the 5, placing it *exactly* where you sense-memorized it at the beginning of the exercise. If you lose the placement, start from the 5 again and descend. You may have to hit the 5 alone a few times until you are sure of where you feel it.

Once you think you have it, try descending again, then start back up and see if you can place the ascending 5 in exactly the same place you started it at when you began descending.

All the same sensations from the previous exercise apply to this one. The only difference is that you are now adding the ascent and descent. All starting notes on the ascent (meaning the 1) must feel as if they begin at palate level. Do not drop below mouth level on these notes or you won't be able to get to the 5 without pulling, pushing, or straining.

As you go higher on your first descent (54321), all starting notes (this means the 5) should be imagined as starting higher up at the back of the head and over the top of the soft palate. These same sensations will also apply as you ascend to the 5 and come back down again. Again, always make sure that the starting notes (the 1) on the ascending section of this exercise feel like they originate on the palate and stay at mouth level.

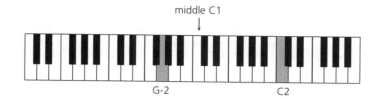

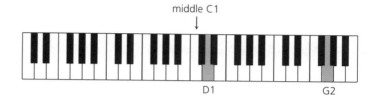

A Reminder About Straining, Squeezing, and Pushing

If you feel strain at any time, it means that you are squeezing or pushing and probably stuck in your throat (because it is not open). Start over, in the area with which you are struggling—even start a couple of notes further down from that area, in order to recapture the right sensations. Always go back to visualizing where everything should be felt and shaped, and where you know the air should feel like it's originating from.

There should be no breaking. The voice will start thinning the higher you go, but it should not break or flip registers. It will take a lot of concentration to keep imagining your vowel taking shape in the oral pharynx and above, the higher you go (and as if the air shoots straight from the back of the head to the front of the face on each successive note).

This is not an easy exercise. There is a great tendency to squeeze the cords together and push out the air as you go higher. Most singers start squeezing in order to keep from breaking, or to keep that edgy sound, but this is incorrect and can lead to damage. You must feel the airflow, but also be mindful not to blow it all out. It's tricky, but not impossible; it just takes focused concentration and learning how to separate the diaphragm from the stomach and neck muscles.

Use Every Vowel

Once you master HEY, change the vowel. Our recommendation is to start with the HEY on the 5, really feel it, and then change the vowel while holding out the HEY as you go to the new vowel of your choice.

When changing the vowel, make sure you don't try to change it inside your throat, or with your vocal cords. The shaping of that new vowel must change as if it has started around the oral pharynx and soft palate area. If you get stuck in your throat and start feeling strain, then you didn't change the vowel in the correct place. Start over again, and work with it until you feel the change taking place on and around the oral pharynx and top of the soft palate area, rather than from inside your throat and neck, or with the tightening of your cords.

Just like with all of the other exercises, you must master this exercise with all the vowels, not just one vowel. Once you're successful, you will see how easily all of this transfers into singing songs.

Any and All Vocal Exercises

We'd like to stress that there are hundreds of exercises available to you and that you should feel free to take the information you have been given in this book and apply it to any exercise of your choosing.

Some singers like to take one note at a time, and change from vowel to vowel all in one breath. They do this for two octaves or so, and then come back down again. Some singers like to take three, four, or five notes at a time, and so on. Also, with regard to vocalizing and exercises, things like lip and tongue trills can be very useful. They not only free up facial muscles, but if you can do them in octaves, they help stretch the cords.

There are many books available on vocal technique that also come with CDs, and many of these CD exercises can be helpful, if done correctly. Our best suggestion is to go ahead and get creative with your vocalizing and exercises. Don't limit yourself. However, if you do choose to mix things up, *always* try to get your cords and air to cooperate with one another by practicing many of the things we have suggested here to help you gain control.

The Greatest Keys to Your Success

True success comes from learning how not to grab your neck muscles, vocal cords, or stomach muscles in any way during any exercise, then learning how not to grab when singing the words and notes of your songs. The body must remain like a wind instrument. If you try to sing or reach high notes by grabbing your neck muscles, you will feel like you can't do it—like you are strangling yourself.

Grabbing Causes Pushing

If you think of your body as a wind instrument (like a flute), then grabbing the neck or stomach would be the equivalent of putting a wood slat straight across that flute (your body) wherever you have grabbed it, thereby cutting off the air and sound at that point. The air should feel as if it *starts* at the back of your head and shoots straight out to the front of your face on each successive note. (Like a mantra, tell yourself, "From the back of the head to the front of the face.") When that air starts coming out, you cannot hold it in any way, not even for a second. If you do, this will cause what we refer to as "grabbing" the stomach and neck muscles. It means you have held the air for a second and, in so doing, have to push or blast that air out for sound.

Don't Overfill Your Air Tank

To prevent grabbing, don't take in so much air that you "fill up the tank." Otherwise, you'll end up losing most of it fairly quickly, because the cords can't control the flow if there is too much air sitting underneath them. The cords *have* to be able to control that flow of air. True loudness comes from cord stretch, cord vibration, and resonance—not blasting air.

To get a handle on the action needed between the air and the cords, try drawing in your air as if you were imitating a dog panting (at the back of your mouth). Don't take it all the way down into your stomach, or you will end up with too much. Once you've drawn it in, it should immediately shoot back out (like a boomerang) from that spot (the back of your throat inside the mouth) as sound is added at the exact same moment you've drawn the air in: *at the tail end of that drawn-in breath.* It has to be done as if the whole event is one simultaneous action—no starting, holding the breath (stopping it), and then starting to sing. You can't take your air in and stop or hold it for one split second. If you do this, it will cause you to close your throat (or squeeze it), and then push.

You can try sitting with yourself and taking only one note—any note (perhaps an easy note for yourself)—and seeing how long you can hold that note out. By doing this, you may be able to *feel* whether you are trying to push your air through the cords for sound. You may also be able to feel whether you took too much air in and were forced to release most of it because of the pressure it created underneath the cords. (This would also mean that you closed your throat for a second before expelling your air and sound.)

Use Your Mind

Learning how to sing correctly is mostly mind over matter. You have to take control of your mind by talking to your voice and telling it what to do on every note in every exercise. You have to trick yourself by using your mind to tell your voice that the air and sound must start from above (inside your head, straight back in the mouth around the oral pharynx/soft palate/back of hard palate area), and not from below (inside the throat or from deep down within the stomach).

You may not be successful at achieving this action for a while. You may still find yourself taking in too much air, closing your throat, or grabbing the stomach and punching it in to push the air up to get the sound out. But rest assured, if you tell your voice something over and over again long enough—telling it what you know it *should* be doing rather than what it has been doing—it will begin to obey your commands. It won't be able to fight *your will* anymore.

The mind is meant to be your servant, not your ruler. And when it comes to learning how to sing *correctly*, it often doesn't act as your friend. If you don't train your mind by repeatedly telling the voice what to do every step of the way, it will instinctively tell you to do things that only hurt your voice, ruin your sound, and mess up your style.

Proper Placement Makes Proper Singing

Pay attention to what you feel when you practice. Going slowly might really help you to diagnose your problem(s). Always try to make sure your vowel shape is not only staying true to the vowel on every note of every exercise (until you reach only the highest of notes in your register, then you may have to modify), but also that those vowels are shaped around the oral pharynx/soft palate/back of hard palate (not so much with the mouth, lips, teeth, jaw, or tongue).

The mouth, lips, teeth, jaw, tongue, and palate usage are end results of proper shaping and placement of the vowels back inside the mouth around the oral pharynx/soft palate/back of hard palate area. Don't try to shape or pronounce the vowels from inside the throat with your cords or neck muscles. This creates squeezing that will, in turn, force you to push air through the cords, because sound won't come out unless the air strikes the cords. If you are squeezed shut to begin with, you can see why you'd have to push the air through to get the sound out. Try, as best you can, to concentrate on beginning the sound, pronouncing and shaping each vowel as if it originates around the oral pharynx/soft palate/back of hard palate area, and then heads toward the front of the face with each successive note.

Then, when you start singing songs, try to do the same thing: shape the words of that song with your articulators (the tongue, lips, teeth, and palate) and inside the mouth—not inside the throat with the neck muscles and vocal cords. Don't pronounce consonants by trying to use your neck muscles or the cords inside of the throat. It's the consonants that are shaped by the lips, teeth, tongue, and hard palate, and not with the throat (between the cords).

If you can master these things, it will change the way you've been singing and feeling about your voice forever. You will no longer be struggling with your throat, body, or air anymore. Best of all, you will find yourself capable of singing anything—*anything*.

SECTION III:
STYLES OF SINGING

By the time you reach this section, you should have repeated the exercises enough times so that you are very familiar with the sensations that need to take place inside the mouth, on the palate, and in the mask.

Your Body Shouldn't Work to Pronounce Words

As we get into singing styles, it's important to learn how to pronounce the words of a song with *only* the tongue, lips, teeth, and palate, to use your face for bracing tension, and to keep your mouth fairly open when singing, so the neck or stomach muscles don't do the work for you.

You must learn to enunciate with only these four articulators. Don't try to pronounce all your consonants inside the throat with the cords, neck, or stomach (unless you are going after a desired effect in a song). This means you need to learn how to use primarily your mouth and its articulators (the tongue, teeth, lips, and palate) to form the consonants.

Sometimes it's not easy to form words this way—especially if you are used to doing things with your body to grab hold of the consonants. But the idea here is to learn how to sing *without* using your body as much as you have been, so that you can free your expression—emotionally, physically, and artistically. If your vocal cord mechanism and the articulators do most of the work, this sets the body free to move (and maybe even dance!).

Some Styles Require You to Break This Rule and Use Your Body

With certain styles, you may have to rely on some body effort for specific sounds (depending on the effects you are trying to achieve). For instance, in a style like jazz, you often try to mimic the sound of an instrument, which may require that you lower (or raise) your larynx, use your neck muscles, or dig down into the stomach for those sounds.

If you have to use your body for effects, you must have complete command over the vocal cord mechanism and how it works *with* the diaphragm. But you must *also* know your body well enough to be able to jump back into the right way of singing (bringing the voice back up into face using all the sensations associated with that; and being capable of using all the feelings and sensations that are to be felt on—and above—the palate, inside the head).

In today's world, the lines between each style of singing often blur. How a vocalist approaches a song doesn't necessarily stay true to its genre like it once did.

However, some keys still exist for certain styles, and they can help you to define which style (or styles) a performer may be using.

Today we now have crossover styles of music. For example: there's rap/rock/metal, pop/R&B, pop/rock, pop/punk, emo/screamo, pop/country, and still other variations that we (the authors) may not even be familiar with yet. In recent years, country music has borrowed from the R&B/soul vocal styling. It would seem that in today's music world, there is so much crossing over and merging of different singing styles that it's almost a free-for-all out there—anything goes.

Beware: Great Stylists Aren't Always Great Singers

Oftentimes, someone you consider a "great singer" isn't necessarily the best singer. What we mean by that is that some of our finest (technically savvy) singers often aren't the ones who make it "big" in the music industry. They may have decent careers making a living doing what they do best, but, for whatever reason, they aren't our most notable performers. The most notable and famous singers are usually the *stylists*.

These great stylists can do amazing things with their voices and, unfortunately, they sometimes hurt their instruments without even knowing it. Because they were born with a gift—the gift of communication—many of them have never stopped to examine what makes that voice a gift, or what dictates good placement versus using a style of singing that actually injures the voice over time. They sing using their voices as a vehicle to communicate whatever emotion comes to them. Depending on the emotion, this may involve squeezing, screaming, manufacturing gravel or rasp, pushing, and improper placement to achieve an effect.

Because of all the crossover singing styles and voice misuse, we have made the decision to stick to the basic styles. We will try to give away the proper (and improper) techniques to help you sing any style, as we cover jazz, country, pop, rock, and R&B.

Jazz

Jazz Song Example

Jazz allegedly traces its origins to the turn of the 20th century in New Orleans, though this unique medium sprung up almost simultaneously in other North American areas, like St. Louis, Kansas City, and Chicago. Traits from West African folk music combined with popular European and light classical music of the late 18th and 19th centuries to create the syncopated rhythms of ragtime and minor chord voicings characteristic of the blues. This powerful combination eventually became the jazz we know today.

Jazz and blues are among America's greatest cultural achievements and contributions to the world community. Born of a multi-hued society, this music unites people across racial, regional, and national divisions. It gives powerful voice to the American experience and has been used to make powerful statements about freedom and creativity.

The origins of the word *jazz* are uncertain: the term is rooted in American slang, though various other adaptations have been suggested. The instruments used in marching bands and dance bands at the turn of century became the basic instruments of jazz—brass, reeds, and drums—and these instruments used the Western 12-tone scale.

Jazz is more about tone and accuracy than anything else. It requires you to approach the music as if your voice were a wind, string, or percussion instrument. Yet, for every jazz singer, breath control is as important (if not more so) than tone, since you must learn how to use your body to imitate the sounds of different instruments. Scatting is an important skill to learn, because it involves imitating these instrumental sounds. This means that, as a jazz singer, you must have complete command of your body (know the different feeling and sensations that create those sounds) as well as complete command of your voice (the vocal cord mechanism), because in jazz, you must be able to jump from one register to the next with 100 percent accuracy.

Jazz singers are seen more as *instrumentalists* than straight singers, while crooners are more famous for the tone of their voices and how they wrap that tone around every word. The focus for jazz is not only on tonal accuracy, but also on pitch accuracy, instrumentation, and chord voicings (harmonies, theory, and chords). Most jazz singers excel at reading music and sight singing, especially since how you sing a song has much more to do with the music than lyrics. The challenge: learning how to sing around much more complicated chord structures and improvising.

What separates jazz from all other styles is that it is the most sophisticated and harmonically challenging style of music. You have to be able to swing as well as any instrumentalist, sing in different time signatures, stylize and interpret a lyric in time or with *rubato*, scat like an instrumentalist, and have the flexibility and creativity to be spontaneously in the moment. Jazz continually challenges singers to reach for a higher level of musicianship and to improve their level of dynamics, diction, musicality, and technical capabilities.

For a jazz singer, it's important to listen to instrumentalists as well as other singers. That is one of the most important things you can do to discover your own voice and style. Jazz music uses blue notes, syncopation, swing, call and response, polyrhythms, and improvisation among its many stylistic markers, while time and feel is also of utmost importance.

Specifics of Jazz

1. In general, jazz is sung in the mask, but not as far forward as pop or rock. The column of air feels more vertical, as opposed to the horizontal sensation felt in the mask when singing pop or country. Jazz comes from a light blended voice (not to be confused with breathiness). You have to use your cords, just not as heavily. The jazz sound doesn't rely on a heavy chest voice like some of the other styles do.

2. The vowels are round, soft, and smooth. The placement should be clean and exact; keeping the mouth in a smile-like position often helps with this. The tongue stays relaxed as it rests up against the lower front teeth, unless you need to use it differently to achieve an effect.

3. Words are usually placed around the soft palate/pharynx area, and the consonants are articulated using the tongue, teeth, lips, and palate (unless you need to use your body to achieve a desired instrumentalist-type effect).

4. Some jazz singers don't have bridged voices and, because of their styling, they manage to get around their breaking points. However, if you want the option of keeping things smooth, it's best to get that voice bridged so you can do both.

5. Scatting is actual vowels, consonants/words, and sounds spread over multiple notes that are usually not connected. Scatting allows for more tonal freedom, spontaneity, and creativity. It is a spontaneous creation of a new melody and rhythm over an established set of chord changes. Melismas (single syllables spread over multiple notes) stay fairly structured and the sound remains connected.

Country

CD • Track 31

Country Song Example

Country music, once known as country and western, is a popular musical form developed in the southern United States, with roots in traditional folk music, spirituals, and the blues. Traditionally accompanied by violin, guitar, banjo, and steel guitar (invented in 1885 in Honolulu), country much later incorporated drums and bass.

Lyrically and musically, country is less complicated than the other genres. In general, it's about storytelling. In addition to the instrumental textures and accents, it's up to the vocalist to add the story's personality. Depending on the song, you do different techniques to achieve different goals. Breath control is important, as is vowel placement, but more than anything, don't forget the twang!

Country has the furthest forward placement of any genre discussed in this book, but that placement is not completely *in* the nose. With its Southern origins, country's prominent twang is as important to the style as breathing is to living. Feel the column of air in the front of the mask, with the back of your throat open and full. If you're even slightly tight or closed, you are too far forward.

In early country and western music, *yodeling* was used to accent the music. Yodeling is an ancient form of calling which uses sudden alterations of vocal register from a low-pitched chest voice to high falsetto tones sung on vowel sounds, almost like a primitive form of scat singing. Yodels create distinct breaks at the moment of transition between the head and chest registers. (This is what gives a yodel its character.) In modern country music, yodels can be heard as more of an accent on the end of a word or phrase.

Early country had a more open vowel placement, with the middle of the tongue raised to achieve the "drawl." The male singers traditionally had a rounder or warmer tone to their voices and the women were more "lilting." In the 50's, rockabilly (a subgenre of rock and country) came onto the scene with its mix of post-war country boogie, hillbilly, and rhythm and blues, bringing with it a new approach to bass playing and rhythmically influencing the vocals. Artists like Elvis Presley, Carl Perkins, and Jerry Lee Lewis are good examples of rockabilly. Currently, modern country singers have started borrowing from the stylings of R&B (Rascal Flatts, LeAnn Rimes), adding yet another flavor to the voice and story.

Again, this style of music requires an ease and knowledge of your own instrument so that you can tell the stories well and with sincerity. There's an old joke that the only way to write a good country song is by having a broken down truck, to be standing in the rain, to watch your mama dying, to have a broken heart, etc. This may be funny, but those lyrics still have to be true to your sound and emotions; you still have to be convincing. The key is: conversation, and learning when to sing and when to speak. You have to remember that you're telling a story and, although you are singing it, the song is more about what you're saying than how you sound. You don't have to be an amazing vocalist. However, you do have to know your instrument well enough to perform and sing the style.

Specifics of Country

1. Country is sung in the mask and almost sounds nasal. The twang is achieved partially from this placement, partly in how you pronounce the vowels and consonants. The column of air is felt more forward/horizontal. Hold the voice in speaking tone placement, and use a little more cord effort than you do in jazz. You almost literally speak, but with a melody (sustained speech, telling the story with melody). Achieve the drawl by raising the back of each side of the tongue up to the molars and jutting back a bit in a rolling motion (as in the word "y'all"). Raise the middle of your tongue a bit, which will incorporate the swallowing muscles.

2. The vowels are open in the back of the throat, and then narrow as the air and tone is leaned toward the front of the mouth. Each vowel is extremely modified into what is called a *diphthong* (a combination of two blends of vowels) depending on the word and how you want to end the phrase (more open if going for a high more belt-like sound; much more closed in the low registers). A good rule of thumb is to always feel the air striking the front of your hard palate. If you feel this, then you'll know you're moving in the right direction.

3. The vowel AH should feel like you're drawing in a refreshing drink of water. A slight EE is usually heard and added at the end of that AH sound (the EE added like a sigh of contentment). The mouths stays open and in a horizontal "smile" position. The soft palate will rise slightly as the air passes through your mouth. OO is usually a blend of the EE and OO vowels (you = ewe).

4. Words are placed forward and in the mask, bordering on entering the nasal area. Consonants are more closed and bitten off. For example, R's are held in the back of the mouth around the molars with the tongue slightly raised, with the mouth staying slightly open.

5. This style takes speech-level placement and phrasing. Record your first time through a song. Then play it back and listen for sections where you could speak the sound more. Record the second time through, this time performing as if you were speaking (like sustained speech) while trying to keep the melody intact. Play it back and listen for sections that could use a more melodic approach. Your job after that is to make the transitions sound effortless—as if they are your own. You may also want to listen to country artists and mimic them exactly. Pay attention to how they phrase. Tape yourself! This style sounds easy to do, but it is not. Listen back to your voice on tape and become the coach.

R&B or Rhythm and Blues

R&B Song Example

Rhythm and blues music, also known as R&B, combines such genres as jump blues, jazz, rock and roll, gospel, Latin, doo-wop, soul , funk, disco, and rap. The term rhythm and blues was originally coined as a marketing term in the United States in 1949 to identify the rocking style of music combining the 12-bar blues and boogie-woogie formats (which later became a fundamental element to rock and roll). Its basic instrumentation is: drums, electric bass, guitar, piano/organ, and vocals.

By the seventies, "rhythm and blues" was being used as a blanket term to describe soul and funk. Like most music of this time, sociopolitical awareness and a philosophical inquiry into the meaning of life (or simply the enjoyment of life) came into focus. Music in general was growing up and taking chances.

Today, the abbreviation R&B is almost always used instead of the term rhythm and blues. This contemporary version can be distinguished by its slick, electronic production style, drum machine–backed rhythms, and smooth, lush vocal arrangements. Uses of hip-hop–inspired beats are typical, although the roughness and grit inherent in hip-hop are usually smoothed out.

Musically and vocally, R&B relies extensively on tonal variations over the course of a performance to keep the listeners' interest and to imply emotion. Along with the instrumentalists, R&B singers often alternate between gentle, breathy, and smooth to harsh, heavy, and raspy tones. This gives the music a wide range of emotional expression. There is a lot of character and sensuality to the voice. The vocalist will change registers quite often, jumping from falsetto to chest voice, and changing their placement to gain effect. The tongue, swallowing muscles, and laryngeal movement (dropping the larynx to achieve a heavier, more throaty sound) are quite often used.

There's a wonderful freedom and comfort in the way the singer flows through melodies and ad-libs (also known as melismas or runs). Until recently, this has been specific to R&B, although elements such as tone and melody choice could be heard in other genres. Country music has recently adopted the licks and runs more commonly associated with R&B. "Old school" R&B vocals have less movement in the way of melismas, and the tonality tends to be more open with the column of air felt in the mask.

The newer approach is full of movement (melismas), which is almost as important as the melody and lyric. To achieve this effect, you use the back of your tongue and the swallowing muscles to squeeze your vocal cords together.

A Quick Tip on Ad-libs, Melismas, and Runs

Although we don't claim to be the definitive experts in this area, we've learned that most runs are manipulated by using vibrato and breath. So, the notes change with the swing of the cord as it naturally vibrates. To practice this, start slowly. First, find a comfortable note and sing AH. Note your vibrato. Is it fast or slow? Does it feel even and smooth? If so, good; if not, practice until it does. Then, take the scale 54321 and sing using the vowel AH on that same comfortable note you started on, and descend. Make sure your voice is being carried all in one breath. Then start again, only this time try to go a little faster. Do this over and over again, gradually bringing in more of your vibrato. This is not an easy exercise, so take your time.

Vocally, R&B is challenging. You really have to be a good stylist and you must have total control over the vocal cord mechanism itself. The way the singer moves through notes with ease and speed requires a good warm-up; an absolute physical understanding and knowledge of your instrument, how it works, and what you can and cannot do with it; and learning how to do ad-libs and runs correctly. Basically, you have to have good vocal health and technique. If you're not making conscious choices on when to squeeze, grab, or even push for effect, you are setting yourself up for future damage.

Because R&B is so diverse in its combination of textures and stylings, we will just cover the basics.

Specifics of R&B

1. R&B is sung in the mask with a speaking-voice placement. This allows you to move through melodies and runs more freely. The column of air is more vertical, somewhere in between jazz and country. Your soft palate must expand from side to side for a more open tone. You can do this by placing your vowels around your oral pharynx/soft palate/back of hard palate area, and by articulating your words with the four articulators. Use a light, blended voice with colorings of rasp, and cord weight or heavier tones thrown in for emotional effect. Although the voice is usually bridged, the singer will often jump back and forth between the chest voice and the head voice.

2. The vowels move back and forth between "round and soft" and "forward and harsh," depending on what effect you want. On higher notes, the vowels are commonly more forward (directly behind the mask), while they move further back onto the soft palate for lower notes. The mouth is shaped—for the most part—in a smile, and the tongue is relaxed and resting behind the teeth.

3. Depending on what you're trying to achieve, words are placed forward in the mask, as if you were speaking (but not as far forward as country placement), accenting each word with a lick (melisma or run) on the end of the phrase. To achieve the low, throaty sound you hear when a singer drops suddenly to a low note, pull your words/vowels back into your soft palate, drop your larynx, and relax your vocal cords and sing a note (preferably a low note, but you can have the same effect on higher notes—just not as high up as you would with a blend).

4. Depending on the desired effect, the pronunciation of words tends to be more horizontal. For a stronger belt sound, the vowel AH sounds more like the "a" in the word "lack." OH leans more toward the vowel AH and its placement. For a softer, airier tone, the placement is more of a classical (vertical) placement, like the AH in the word "father," and OH in the word "home."

5. Take chances with your voice by playing with tone, range, grunts, growls, whispers, coos, and other things, and always tape yourself! You'll be a better singer for it.

Rock

CD • Track 33

Rock Song Example

Rock 'n' roll emerged in the United States in the late 1940s. It got its name in the 1950s from DJ Alan Freed, who used it to describe the rollicking R&B music of the time.

Rock has been one of the most popular forms of music in the western world. At its heart is the rhythm, which was (but has evolved from) basically a boogie-woogie blues rhythm with an accentuated backbeat, almost always on snare drum. It's typically played with two electric guitars (one lead, one rhythm), an electric bass guitar, and a drum kit. Keyboards are a common addition to the mix. In its earliest form, the piano was the lead instrument.

"Rocking" was a term first used by gospel singers in the South to mean something similar to spiritual rapture, and in the 1940s, the term "rock 'n' roll" took that term and gave it another meaning. It then became used as a double entendre to refer to dancing but with the hidden subtext of sex. Later, it evolved into the various subgenres of what is now simply called rock. Its huge success in the United States made ripples across the Atlantic, culminating in 1964 with the British Invasion.

While rock musicians typically write their own material, many of the early hits were covers of earlier R&B or blues songs. Eventually, all of these characteristics—belting, squeezing, rasp, talking, and hoots—were incorporated into what we now know as rock singing. Blues proved to be a big influence on some of the most influential artists of the 1960s, such as Led Zeppelin, Cream, Janis Joplin, Jimi Hendrix, and the Yardbirds (defining the vocal sound all the more).

Rock 'n' roll is rebellious, and the vocalist is expected to be its larger-than-life representative. It can be angry, cheeky, sexual, and fun—sometimes all at once. Adding in the sexual subtext and rapture of the earliest form of rock with R&B and blues, this combination of elements shapes the tone of how the rock singer is not only seen, but *sounds*. Whether it's emo, metal, punk, classic, modern rock, or whatever subgenre, the voice is expected to convey that attitude. To be a good rock singer, you have to have a certain swagger, and—for lack of a better word—"balls," both in how you carry yourself and how you sing. You're competing to be heard over a band and sometimes a rowdy audience. To do that, you have to project your voice and place it where it will cut through the easiest: in the mask at speech level, with an open throat. Breath control is also very important in maintaining a consistently strong sound—especially since you will be expected to run around on stage. A lot of rock singers keep in shape by jogging and doing a lot of cardio to maintain good control of their breathing.

Traditionally, the singers became sex symbols (such as Robert Plant, Donovan, Jim Morrison, and Jimi Hendrix), and technique wasn't high on the list of important factors. However, convincingly expressed emotion was, and still is, high on that list. Today's modern rock singers may not have the greatest of ranges, but most of them do try to take care of their instruments, due to the physical demands put on the voice.

Today, rock vocals have a certain edge, power, freedom of expression, and aggression giving them their distinct tone, regardless of lyrical content.

A Quick Tip on Screaming

This can be a very damaging vocal effect and does not come easy to a person unfamiliar with this style of singing. We highly recommend taking things slowly, when learning how to scream. That said, here are a few suggestions to achieving that particular sound:

There are several types of screams in rock music, and they all begin with proper airflow and placement. Start by shaping your mouth in a slight smile. Now starting very quietly, say AH (like in the word "lack," but don't raise up your soft palate). Instead of making it clean, add enough air to whisper. Don't sing a pitch yet. Pay attention to where you feel the air. Is it striking the middle of the hard palate and expanding back towards the soft palate? If so, it's right. If not, keep trying. Now add a little cord stretch so the voice sounds as if it's "soft crackling." If your air placement has changed, stop and try again until you can consistently make that crackling sound and keep your air placement. Now you are ready to play with pitch and words. *If your voice hurts or feels strained in any way: **stop**, rest, and try again another day.*

A Word from Tita on the Merits of Mucus

Mucus or phlegm: most people cringe at these words but, in my experience, in some cases a little mucus can go a long way. That isn't to say that you should go out and eat the entire dairy section at your local grocer. What I am saying is that you are never going to be in a vocally perfect situation, so be prepared for anything, and use it to your advantage. If you find you have mucus and are about to sing a song that requires screaming, lighten the amount of cord effort and add a bit more breath pressure without losing your placement. This is a *slight* adjustment. *Do not push!*

Specifics of Rock

1. Rock is sung in the mask at speech-level, which allows you the freedom to use breath pressure and cord stretch for effect. It uses both of these effects a lot. Like R&B, rock uses colorings of rasp, gravel, weight of cord, and breath pressure for any given effect. The column of air is vertical and slightly forward. To achieve the proper placement, the throat must be relaxed and open. It should feel as if it is an open tube for air to travel through. Both classic and modern styles of rock singing use the neck and proper use of the air from the support of the diaphragm to achieve power. Although many current artists do not have bridged voices, due to the physical nature of this style, we would suggest that you do. Many singers typically sound just as strong in their head voice as they do in their chest voice, which can cause future damage to the voice, if you are not in right placement.

2. The vowels are forward, and move back and forth from the hard to soft palate. They are articulated with the tongue, lips, teeth, and palate—often at speech level—and can sound harsh. The tonality should sound like your speaking voice to help you cut through and be heard over a band. It also adds a certain edgy quality that's associated with this particular style. For the most part, the mouth is shaped in a smile, and the tongue is relaxed. You may feel the air in your mouth take form, like that of a potato or marshmallow sitting in the middle of your mouth. Like R&B, this genre relies on different vocal effects to convey emotion. As we said earlier in the book, this is a lighter sound than you would expect. Cord effort will vary depending on the effect you are going for. Try reading the lyrics out loud and projecting them forward without tightening or squeezing.

3. Depending on what you'd like to achieve, word pronunciation tends to be more horizontal (like R&B). Since you are usually belting, AH becomes more like the "A" in the word "lack" and OH stays in AH placement. EE is pronounced like the IH sound in the word "this." EH and OO are formed with a smile shape to the mouth. Of all the styles, rock should almost always be felt in the mask. To strengthen the voice without straining, try saying "HEY" or "HO" on a pitch in the middle of your range. Keep the vowels on the front of the hard palate while maintaining an open relaxed throat (like a tube for air to travel through). Now, add a little volume, as if you were trying to shout. Pay attention to your throat: did you squeeze or tighten up? If you tightened, try again until you are successful. Carefully go higher in pitch, repeating this exercise.

4. *Always* warm up before you sing and warm down afterwards! This is a given for any genre, but especially when singing rock. The physical demands are great, so get into the habit of it. Your voice will last a lot longer if you do.

Pop Music

CD • Tracks 30-33

(All Songs): Pop Song Examples

The term pop music describes what is most popular on the radio circuit. It denotes specific stylistic traits, particularly the use of catchy melodies, formulaic song structure, or lush ballads and rhythms. Rock, hip-hop, dance, country, and almost any other genre can be considered pop, making it a very flexible category. All of the song examples we have in this book are a representation of pop in various genres, each having a particular mainstream quality to them. Because pop is so diverse, you may want to incorporate a lot of the specifics we already talked about in the previous styles.

Pop music consumers are pretty wide in age range, but are primarily teens, and the music is marketed to that demographic. This strategy began in the fifties and sixties and is the driving force behind pop music. Because of this, record companies look for a brighter, more youthful tonal quality in the voice as well as a youthful, hip image. That vocal quality has been taken and refined into the smooth and cleaner tones created by such singers as Barbra Streisand, Michael Bolton, and Celine Dion (for the soft rock and adult contemporary categories).

Music videos, merchandise, CDs, commercials, live performances, and television shows such as *American Idol* are all used to advertise (or create) the artist (and vice versa), helping to build excitement while also keeping the performer in the public eye.

To give you an idea of how pop crosses over into other genres, below is a list of pop artists through the years starting in the fifties, when the music began separating itself from other styles. A lot of these artists overlap into the next era, so this list is a generalization. If you are unfamiliar with some of the older artists, we recommend looking them up. You'll hear a lot their influences in the music of today:

1950s: Bing Crosby, Frank Sinatra, Dean Martin, Nat King Cole, Fats Domino, and Elvis Presley.

1960s: The Beatles, Rolling Stones, Gene Pitney, Carol King, Neil Diamond, Lulu, Aretha Franklin, Sam Cooke, Stevie Wonder, Ray Charles, Bob Dylan, Marvin Gaye, and Simon and Garfunkel.

1970s (the decade of disco): Abba, the Bee Gees, Billy Joel, Elton John, the Eagles, Rod Stewart, Fleetwood Mac, Cat Stevens, the Jackson Five, Roberta Flack, Earth, Wind and Fire, and KC and the Sunshine Band.

1980s: Michael Jackson (the "King of Pop"), Madonna, Prince, Janet Jackson, Cyndi Lauper, Duran Duran, U2, A-Ha, Whitney Houston, Lionel Ritchie, Rick Springfield, Wham (George Michael), Milli Vanilli, and Culture Club.

1990s: Even though a lot of these acts started in the mid-to-late '80s, R&B pop acts took a more dominant role on the radio with Mariah Carey, Boyz II Men, En Vogue, Brandy, TLC, and the rap act Salt n' Peppa. Boy/girl acts also came to the forefront with New Kids on the Block, New Edition (late '80s/early '90s), Backstreet Boys, Hanson, 'N Sync, and the Spice Girls. The late '90s saw the rise of Latin pop with Ricky Martin, Jennifer Lopez, Shakira, Enrique Iglesias, and Marc Anthony.

2000s: Hip-hop blended with pop, with artists such as Eminem, Nelly, 50 Cent, and Ludacris, and on a subtler note Beyonce Knowles, Justin Timberlake, Nelly Furtado, and Christina Aguilera. Mariah Carey and Madonna made incredible comeback records. Teen pop artists dominating the charts were Britney Spears, Hillary Duff, Lindsay Lohan, and Ashley Simpson. There were also pop/punk artists such as Avril Lavigne and Green Day and, of course, *American Idol* sensation Kelly Clarkson.

Specifics of Pop

1. This style is sung in the mask. It's probably the brightest and cleanest of tones in all the genres (although it does depend on what subgenre you might be singing). Generally, the placement is behind the nose, but not as far forward as country. The quality is light, but not airy. The sound should be at speech-level (exactly the same as your speaking voice). It should feel as if air is circling around the middle of your hard palate, and have a very slight "whine-like" tone to it.

2. The vowels are bright and pronounced, as if you were speaking them (keeping your mouth in the smile position helps). An additional way to achieve this is to read aloud while projecting your voice forward without pushing, straining, or squeezing. Start by allowing the phrase you are reading aloud to begin at the top of your breath as you exhale, and try to keep it evenly supported until it's finished. At first, this may be difficult, so go slowly and concentrate on relaxing your throat, keeping the placement forward, and projecting your voice into the pocket above the hard palate (without shouting it into there). This exercise will also work for most of the other styles described in this book.

3. Words are usually placed on the hard palate. The consonants of every word are articulated using the tongue, teeth, lips, and palate—not with your neck muscles, vocal cords/throat, or stomach muscles.

4. This style requires a bridged voice to achieve the clean, clear tonality—regardless of the genre.

5. Depending on the genre, melismas can be used in the same way R&B/gospel accentuates the ends of phrases.

APPENDIX A
Acid Reflux and Vocal Abuse Disorders

What You Should Know about Acid Reflux

Every singer should know that acid reflux is a very serious and under-diagnosed disease; *80 percent of all singers have acid reflux*. Yes, that's right: 80 percent! So, what is acid reflux, and why are singers more prone to it than any other group of people? To answer that, it's important to know some anatomical and physiological things about the diaphragm and stomach, and how these two body parts interact—especially in singers.

Anatomically, the diaphragm is a partition of muscles and tendons between the chest and abdominal cavity (or midriff) that's located just above the stomach. The stomach is a pear-shaped bag located between the esophagus and the intestines. It lies cross-wise in the abdominal cavity beneath the diaphragm. Food enters the stomach from the esophagus via a muscular sphincter. This sphincter—the connection between the esophagus and the stomach—is supposed to prevent food from passing back up the esophagus. Inside the stomach, gastric juices (known as pepsin and acid) break down the food for digestion. The seepage of acid creeping back up into the esophagus via that muscle sphincter is referred to as acid reflux.

Singers use their diaphragms considerably more than most other people: a constancy of in, out, and of pushing downward. Over time, this usage can weaken the sphincter muscle between the esophagus and stomach. Once the muscle has weakened or you produce excessive amounts of acid for any number of reasons, the acid can then regurgitate and travel as far up as the vocal cord and nasal passage level (known as laryngeal/pharyngeal reflux). This regurgitation may cause burning and swelling (with congestion as a result), and may also cause excessive mucus on the cords and in the nasal passages.

It might never occur to you that the congestion could be caused by something like reflux, because symptoms vary from person to person. Some people wake up each morning heavily congested thinking it's just allergies or the onset of a cold. Upon arising, they may constantly need to blow their noses or clear their throats (because they feel like they have mucus, or something else, sitting on the cords). Others can actually feel a burning sensation in the esophagus (heartburn) or a burning sensation between the vocal cords ("a lump in the throat"), soreness (between the cords), or a swelling of the cords (hoarseness or laryngitis) that makes it hard to sing—especially in the upper registers.

Testimonial from Dena Murray

In September of 2005, I lost my voice. It started with a sinus infection, but once the infection was gone, my voice didn't get better. My speaking voice had returned, but not my singing voice. More than one octave was missing from it; nothing but air would come out of my mouth throughout my upper middle to high register, whenever I tried to sing.

After one month of suffering with this, I finally went to a notable laryngologist. He took one look at my vocal cord area and bolted backwards. "Oh my God," he said, "You have severe acid reflux and are very allergic to foods—probably have been all of your life." He then explained to me that, because of the allergies, my stomach was producing so much acid that my body was creating an overabundance of mucus. This mucus was making its way up through my vocal cords and into my nasal passages. The excessive burning, swelling, and subsequent mucus caused from acid and allergies was preventing my arytenoids from being able to stretch back to sing.

I'd known about the allergies. Back in the late eighties, I'd gone to one of the top five allergists in the world. Once the allergist was able to get my inhalants under control (things like tree pollens, mold, grasses, weeds, etc.) by treating me with shots to build up my immune system, he was able to diagnose the source of where it began: foods.

Unfortunately, back then, no one knew much about acid reflux. They didn't have today's technology to see and diagnose such things, let alone the ability to prescribe medication for it. So there wasn't much my allergist could do for me about this condition except teach me how to rotate the foods I was allergic to, so that my immune system wouldn't weaken so much.

I was able to get a handle on it for about ten years, but soon thereafter I started feeling and noticing that I was getting hoarse from time to time, maybe lasting a day or two at time. It was scaring me. Every time it happened, I couldn't help but wonder if it was a technique problem (at the time I'd been learning how to "belt," and was practicing a lot). But always, after a day or two of hoarseness, my voice would miraculously come back completely—three octaves and then some. That's when I'd start rationalizing and tell myself, "Maybe it *isn't* my technique." I was afraid to go to the laryngologist, afraid of what he might find, and afraid it would mean my technique was faulty.

It went like this for a couple of years. Obviously, it wasn't happening enough to really frighten me into seeing that specialist. Not until that sinus infection in 2005 did I get scared enough to do something about it. Because, this time, it made me lose a big chunk of my singing voice, and not for just a couple of days—it turned into weeks.

The laryngologist explained that when people get sick with infection, they produce something called *histamine* (a word most everyone is somewhat familiar with because of the antihistamines available to purchase over the counter for allergies or cold symptoms). He said that for people like myself, histamine wreaks havoc on acid reflux. This is what happened to me when *I* got sick.

Additionally, he told me that cortisone (which I'd been given by my GP along with an antibiotic at the start of this infection) is one of the worst things one can use to get rid of inflammation caused by infection. For people with acid reflux, cortisone and certain antibiotics only create more acid. By this time, it became very clear what had happened to my voice, and that I was in a no-win situation.

He took a culture for sinus infection because he suspected I still had one, though I didn't think so, because I no longer had a sore throat, nor was I producing any yellow or green mucus. I also wasn't having any headaches. My only symptom was that I was still very tired, which I assumed came from the depression I was in over what had been happening to my voice.

When the cultures came back, it turned out that I was wrong! I still had a low-grade bacterial infection. This time, though, instead of pill antibiotic, I was prescribed an antibiotic ointment to apply directly in my nose with a cotton swab, so as not to further upset my gastric juices. Until that day, I had no idea anything like this was even available. The laryngologist also prescribed Protonix (a prescription-only medicine) to be used three times a day for one entire month, and after that, two times a day *for the rest of my life* because of my severe food allergies. Lastly, he warned that it might take *a few months* for my voice to come back and my cords to heal. This part I really did *not* want to hear.

After four and half months (I kid you not), my singing voice finally returned. The good news is that once it returned, *it came back stronger and better than it had ever been in my entire life*. Today, I can honestly tell you that losing my voice when I did, how I did, and for as long as I did, was the best thing that could have ever happened, because it truly turned out to be a blessing in disguise.

I don't know about the rest of you, but I love using my voice to teach singers how to sing correctly. I couldn't imagine losing my career as a voice teacher—one of the things in life I enjoy doing most. That fear alone is what finally prompted me to seek out the best doctors and do everything I was instructed to do. Because of it, I am now enjoying my voice in a way I never have before. My voice consistently works well for me on a daily basis, and I now have a freedom with singing I always knew was possible but couldn't own as the truth until I got treated for what turned out to be the root of the problem—a problem I'd had for at least twenty years and never knew about.

My best advice to anyone who is in doubt about what might be going on with his or her voice: seek out a reputable laryngologist as soon as possible. Don't wait. Don't put yourself through the constant on-again, off-again misery of wondering. Going to a specialist is a much better way to go than continuing to cling to the fear. In the end, you get answers and solutions.

Testimonial from Tita Hutchison

I had no idea that I had acid reflux until I noticed that my range started to shrink and my voice grew tired after a few hours of singing. It sounds logical that anyone would be tired after a few hours of singing, but this was a problem I'd never had before, and I couldn't help but start thinking, "No singer should have this problem if he or she is singing correctly!"

So, terrified that my technique was bad, or that I had nodes or some other terrible malady, I went to see an ear, nose, and throat doctor to get checked out. After lots of poking, prodding, scoping, and all the fun that comes with any doctor visit, he told me that my arytenoids were inflamed due to reflux.

This doctor told me to eat Tums (extra strength), both before going to bed and any time I felt a bit of phlegm (mucus) coming on. He then sent me on my way. He also told me that I should have my tonsils out, but I decided to wait on that. That's an even bigger issue, and I decided to consider it at a later time. My immediate concern was to get my voice working again. I continued to eat a lot of Tums and paid close attention to what I was experiencing inside my throat on every given day.

This whole episode prompted me to become more acutely aware of my body. I could always tell when I was having a good vocal day or a bad one, and I was also learning how to get around the problem on those bad days. I didn't have the normal symptoms for acid reflux like burning and sore throat. I did, however, have an excess of phlegm and congestion on my cords and in my nasal passages in the mornings, which I later discovered is a big red flag.

But why would I only have congestion in the mornings? Well, if you really think about it, it makes sense. You lie flat when you sleep, and everything supposedly relaxes, including that muscle sphincter attached to the esophagus and stomach. If it relaxes and weakens too much, acid starts to make its way back up into the esophagus, throat, and sometimes even into the sinus passages. The acid irritates the membranes in these areas so much that your body starts to produce a lot of mucus to protect those areas from the burning, and upon arising in the morning, you find yourself blowing your nose and feeling like you have to constantly clear your throat just to get things moving so you can start singing.

Soon the Tums weren't doing anything for me anymore and I began using Prilosec. After making my way up to taking four pills a day and barely feeling a result, I admitted to being human. You see, I'd always been hell-bent on *not* being one of those typical "diva" singers. You know the ones I'm talking about. You've seen them sipping their tea with lemon and honey, making strange noises that could be mistaken for snorting, humming, or small animal calls, ingesting gobs of lozenges and throat sprays, worried they won't be able to sing at a certain time of the day, mildly hypochondriac, wearing scarves...

Well, since that time I've come to realize that, whatever issues I had with those types of singers—musical reputation aside—those problems had now become mine, too. There really is something to all that fuss. They are taking care of their instruments, which in the case of the singer is even more important than it is for other musicians, since this instrument can't be replaced. If your cords break down, you can't just go to a music store and buy a new string. When your instrument lives inside of your body and that body part *is* your instrument, you should be aware of every little twitch and learn what to do to take care of it when you know it's not working well.

Finally, after months of struggling, I gave in and sought out a well-known laryngologist. He prescribed Protonix (prescription-only medicine), and I have been happily singing away ever since. So my advice is, "When in doubt, go get yourself looked at." Find a really good vocal specialist. It's worth the money to know, get answers, and be given solutions, and it's not worth the risk of creating more damage.

What You Should Know about Vocal Abuse

Many singers who are born with gifted voices assume that, because they have these gifts, their voices will always be there for them. A singer like this is unconscious as to when he or she may be hurting the voice and will usually only seek counsel when the throat is hurting badly or when things with the voice start going terribly wrong. It's unfortunate that it sometimes takes being backed up against a wall before one goes to a specialist (laryngologist) to find out what's happening. Our purpose here is to give out some information before the damage becomes irreversible. Here are some things you should know about vocal abuse.

Symptoms of Serious Vocal Abuse

- After extensive singing or speaking, the inside of the larynx (where the vocal cords are located) is sore, the voice becomes excessively breathy, you get hoarse after you've been singing for any amount of time, or you lose your voice entirely.

- You can no longer reach your highest notes without getting louder the higher you go and feel like you have more difficulty controlling your voice (having to strain a lot just to sing).

- Even after a few days of complete vocal rest, you are still hoarse or excessively breathy.

- Over time, you've lost range and can't get it back.

Serious Vocal Abuse Disorders

Hoarseness/Laryngitis

This is a rough, scratchy, or breathy quality to the voice. If others can't hear it, you usually can. You can also feel it because, if you're hoarse, you'll find yourself feeling like you have to strain just to get the sound out. It can be caused by growths, swelling, or scarring on the inner edge of the vocal cord(s). Additionally, acid reflux can cause a burning sensation in the throat when singing. This can create swelling as well as a lot of mucus on the cords, and also make you feel like you have to constantly clear your throat (which only irritates things further, because when you clear your throat you are constantly rubbing the cords together). Sometimes, you may have actually cleared off whatever it was but don't know it because of the irritation the rubbing creates. That irritation alone will make you think and feel that you must keep clearing your throat.

Vocal Fatigue

This is the inability to vocalize for a long period of time. It's usually the result of oversinging (*note: it's important to rest a voice as much as possible when doing a lot of back-to-back gigs*). It can also be caused by speaking or singing too loudly, incorrectly, for too long without a break, and from misusing (tensing and squeezing) the neck and abdominal muscles.

Nodules

Nodes are tiny callous-like bumps on the vocal cords. Signs you have nodules include: excessive breathiness, hoarseness, and loss of range. Nodes vary in degree of damage, so, if you are experiencing some or all of these symptoms, you should go to a laryngologist and get scoped (laryngoscopy). Nodes develop from bad habits and poor technique, but they can also develop if acid reflux goes undiagnosed and untreated.

Surgery is not usually recommended for nodes. If caught early enough, it's mostly just a matter of vocal rest, treating the reflux, or taking voice lessons to correct bad habits and achieve better vocal technique. There is such a thing as receding nodes where, with rest, the node or nodes will go down and recede back into the vocal fold.

Polyps

A polyp can occur from one single event—for example, singing very loudly on a note that is too high for you to reach, so you forcefully blow your air to get your voice up and out. A polyp is a lesion that's formed after a blood vessel has broken (similar to a blister). Sometimes acid reflux can cause a polyp and it may only appear on one vocal cord instead of both. Signs of polyps are persistent hoarseness, or an abnormally deep voice that comes on over a period of time (for women, this means sounding like a man). Polyps *do not* go away on their own. Treatment must be sought, and in this case, surgery may be required.

APPENDIX B
The Exercises
(All Twelve Keys)

If you play an instrument, have an accompanist, or can sight-read music, you might find the following reference useful. All exercises are shown in the twelve keys in which they can be performed. Note: When singing the scales in practice, always work within your own vocal range and continue to observe the suggested keys presented in the text and on the CDs.

Pushing and Squeezing Exercises

Exercise for Breaking the Habit of Using the Tongue and Swallowing Muscles

Mask and Bridging Exercise

Exercise for Changing the Vowel

Blending Exercise

Exercise for Changing the Vowel (Blending)

Exercise with the Vowels EH and OH

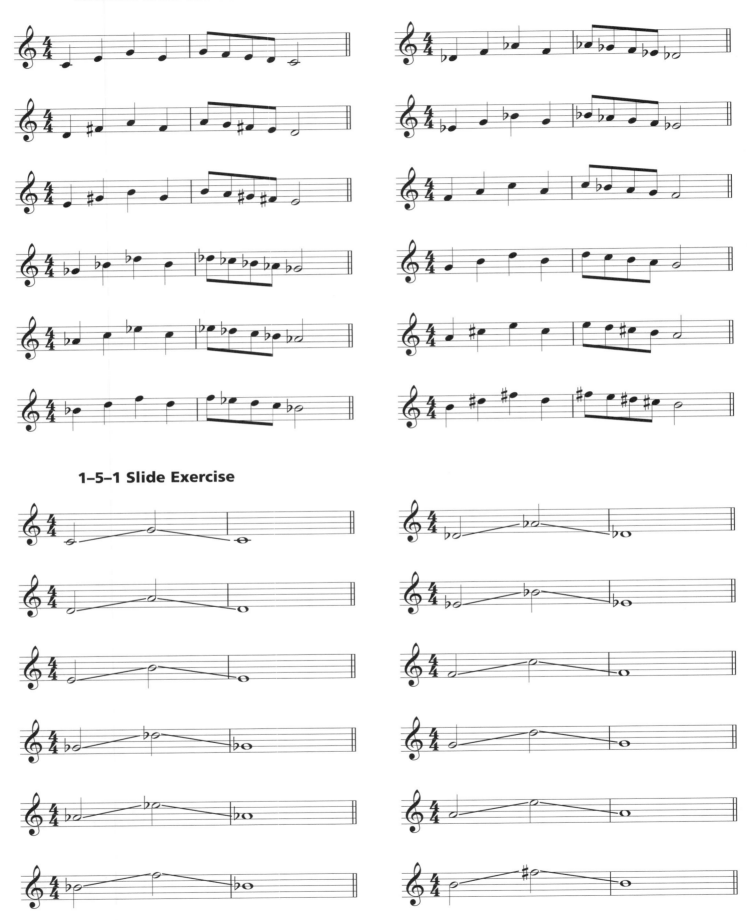

1–5–1 Slide Exercise

1–5, 54321 Slide Exercise

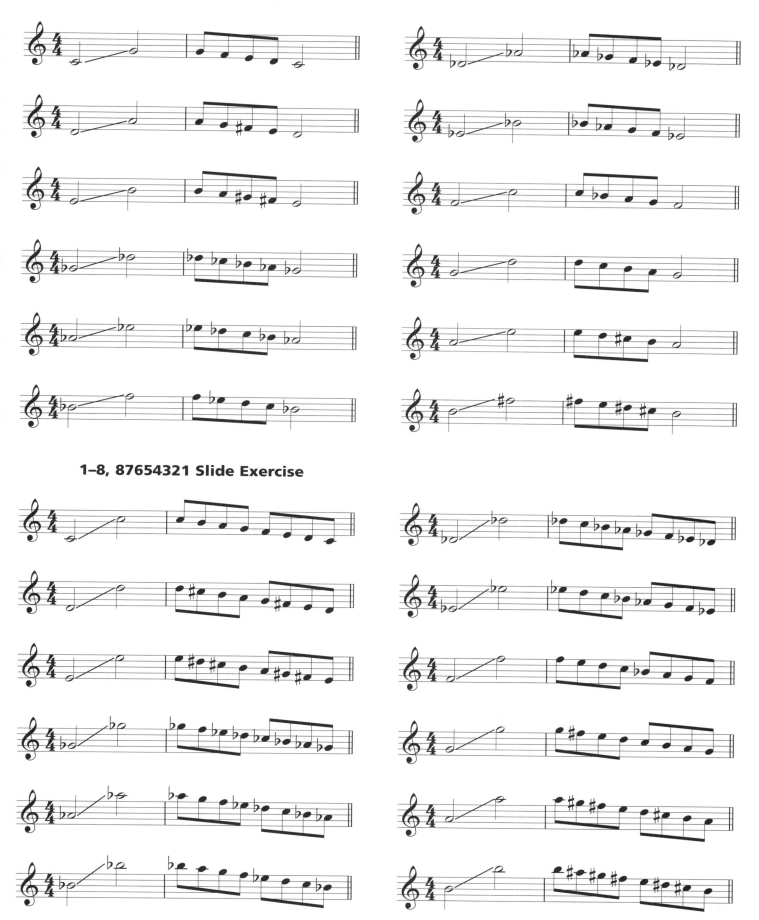

1–8, 87654321 Slide Exercise

1358531 Exercise

HEY Exercise

HEY Exercise #2

CD INDEX

ABOUT THE RECORDING

All songs produced and arranged by Tim Pedersen except for "Down to Nothing," produced by Cranium Music.

All songs written, sung, and arranged by Tita Hutchison.

Guitar, bass, and drums: Tim Pedersen, except for "After Always."

Bass on "After Always": Brian Allen

Male vocals for scales: Kevin Campos

ABOUT THE AUTHORS

Dena Murray

Dena Murray was born in Los Angeles, California, where she began her singing career at age of 12 after having been selected to perform as a soloist in a local recital of Handel's Messiah. With over 25 years of professional experience, her performance career has included musical theater productions, summer stock, Shakespeare festivals, television and motion picture work, and voice-over for radio commercial advertising.

In 1993, Ms. Murray joined the teaching staff of the Musicians Institute in Hollywood, California as a vocal instructor. She served as the head of vocal technique from 1995–2006, and wrote the curriculum for that program.

Since leaving MI, she teaches privately and online (see her website *www.denamurray.com* for more details), working with singers and voice-over talent. Some of her students include voice talent from CBS, NBC, HBO, motion picture documentary films, television commercials, and demo and session artists.

Throughout her professional career, Dena has employed a style of teaching that helps to enhance the self-esteem of her students by creating an environment that inspires creativity while fostering confidence.

In 2002, her first book, *Vocal Technique: A Guide To Finding Your Real Voice*, was released worldwide by Hal Leonard Publications. The culmination of her experiences with hundreds of students, that book contains her vocal technique philosophy and method (why it's important to develop the head and chest registers separately, how to accomplish this, and then how to begin the process of bridging the registers to sound like one).

Advanced Vocal Technique: Middle Voice, Placement, and Styles (co-authored by Tita Hutchison) contains both authors' combined experience in training the voice, and how to apply this technique in all styles of singing.

Dena graduated from Ithaca College, Ithaca, New York, with a Bachelor of Science in Speech.

If you would like to contact Dena for private lessons, online lessons that can be taken from anywhere in the world, or to book a clinic, see her website at ***www.denamurray.com*** for more details.

Dedication from Dena Murray

My collaborative part of this book is dedicated to the memory of my first *real* voice teacher, Helen McComas.

Thank Yous from Dena Murray

To Tita Hutchison for the opportunity to work with her, become friends, and to learn a hell of a lot about the different styles of singing.

To Tim Pedersen for all of his relentless determination, skill, and patience.

To Jeff Schroedl at Hal Leonard Corporation, for his support.

To Chad Johnson, our editor, for his ongoing support and expertise.

I would also like to thank my boyfriend, BT, for every single thing he does for me, his continued support, and love.

Lastly, I would like to give a special thank you to my brother, Andrew Jay Kulick, for helping me to protect the integrity of all my written works.

Tita Hutchison

Tita grew up in Hawaii, where she started her career in musical theater. (Her father is a director/dancer, and her mother is a dancer/choreographer.) Throughout her formative years, she practically *lived* backstage, onstage, and at rehearsal halls.

Tita is a versatile vocalist, equally comfortable in the studio or in a live setting. She's spent her life grooming her performance skills, singing everything from show tunes, rock, R&B, jazz, opera, and blues, to traditional Hawaiian music. (She's also a pretty good hula dancer!) Blending all of these styles together with her own musical abilities, Tita has garnered a reputation not only for her dynamic voice and performances, but also for her willingness to take on any musical challenge that come her way.

She's had the great fortune and privilege of working with musical legends Herbie Hancock and Waylon Jennings, as well top name producers like Keith Forsey, Brian Malouf, and Rick Rubin.

You can hear Tita's voice on commercials, albums, TV, and film, and you can catch her performing in a myriad of projects around the Los Angeles area, as well as all over the U.S.

If you would like to take private lessons with Tita, book her for seminars or clinics that may (or may not) include private one-on-one lessons, or book her for a gig, she can be contacted at titamusic@aol.com or www.myspace.com/titamusic.

Thank Yous from Tita Hutchison

First and foremost I would like to thank Dena Murray for this opportunity, her friendship, her knowledge, and her spirit. You are truly one of a kind, and I'm lucky to know you.

I would also like to thank Tim Pedersen for his support, his talent, and love. You have opened my eyes to a world I never thought possible. I love you. Thank you.

Also, special thanks to my mom, dad, brother, and my extended family Leanne, Masaki, Julia, and Audrey for making me laugh, and having a place in your hearts that I can always call home.

Jeff Schroedl and Chad Johnson for their hard work and support.

And lastly, I'd like to say thank you to all the people who have come through my life, past and present. You have helped me grow with every interaction, no matter how small.

Musicians Institute Press

is the official series of Southern California's renowned music school, Musicians Institute. **MI** instructors, some of the finest musicians in the world, share their vast knowledge and experience with you – no matter what your current level. For guitar, bass, drums, vocals, and keyboards, **MI Press** offers the finest music curriculum for higher learning through a variety of series:

ESSENTIAL CONCEPTS
Designed from MI core curriculum programs.

MASTER CLASS
Designed from MI elective courses.

PRIVATE LESSONS
Tackle a variety of topics "one-on-one" with MI faculty instructors.

KEYBOARD

Blues Hanon
by Peter Deneff • **Private Lessons**
00695708 . . . . $14.95

Dictionary of Keyboard Grooves
by Gail Johnson • **Private Lessons**
00695556 Book/CD Pack $16.95

Funk Keyboards – The Complete Method
by Gail Johnson • **Master Class**
00695336 Book/CD Pack $14.95

Jazz Chord Hanon
by Peter Deneff • **Private Lessons**
00695791 . . . . $12.95

Jazz Hanon
by Peter Deneff • **Private Lessons**
00695554 . . . . $12.95

Jazz Piano
by Christian Klikovits • **Essential Concepts**
00695773 Book/CD Pack $17.95

Keyboard Technique
by Steve Weingard • **Essential Concepts**
00695365 . . . . $12.95

Keyboard Voicings
by Kevin King • **Essential Concepts**
00695209 . . . . $12.95

Music Reading for Keyboard
by Larry Steelman • **Essential Concepts**
00695205 . . . . $12.95

Pop Rock Keyboards
by Henry Sol-Eh Brewer & David Garfield • **Private Lessons**
00695509 Book/CD Pack $19.95

R&B Soul Keyboards
by Henry J. Brewer • **Private Lessons**
00695327 Book/CD Pack $16.95

Rock Hanon
by Peter Deneff • **Private Lessons**
00695784 . . . . $12.95

Salsa Hanon
by Peter Deneff • **Private Lessons**
00695226 . . . . $12.95

Stride Hanon
by Peter Deneff • **Private Lessons**
00695882 . . . . $12.95

DRUM

Afro-Cuban Coordination for Drumset
by Maria Martinez • **Private Lessons**
00695328 Book/CD Pack $14.95

Blues Drumming
by Ed Roscetti • **Essential Concepts**
00695623 Book/CD Pack $14.95

Brazilian Coordination for Drumset
by Maria Martinez • **Master Class**
00695284 Book/CD Pack $14.95

Chart Reading Workbook for Drummers
by Bobby Gabriele • **Private Lessons**
00695129 Book/CD Pack $14.95

Double Bass Drumming
by Jeff Bowders
00695723 Book/CD Pack $19.95

Drummer's Guide to Odd Meters
by Ed Roscetti • **Essential Concepts**
00695349 Book/CD Pack $14.95

Funk & Hip-Hop Grooves for Drums
by Ed Roscetti • **Private Lessons**
00695679 Book/CD Pack $14.95

Latin Soloing for Drumset
by Phil Maturano • **Private Lessons**
00695287 Book/CD Pack $14.95

Musician's Guide to Recording Drums
by Dallan Beck • **Master Class**
00695755 Book/CD Pack $19.95

Rock Drumming Workbook
by Ed Roscetti • **Private Lessons**
00695838 Book/CD Pack $19.95

Working the Inner Clock for Drumset
by Phil Maturano • **Private Lessons**
00695127 Book/CD Pack $16.95

VOICE

Harmony Vocals
by Mike Campbell & Tracee Lewis • **Private Lessons**
00695262 Book/CD Pack $17.95

Musician's Guide to Recording Vocals
by Dallan Beck • **Private Lessons**
00695626 Book/CD Pack $14.95

Sightsinging
by Mike Campbell • **Essential Concepts**
00695195 . . . . $17.95

Vocal Technique
by Dena Murray • **Essential Concepts**
00695427 Book/CD Pack $22.95

OTHER REFERENCE

Approach to Jazz Improvisation
by Dave Pozzi • **Private Lessons**
00695135 Book/CD Pack $17.95

Ear Training
by Keith Wyatt, Carl Schroeder & Joe Elliott • **Essential Concepts**
00695198 Book/2-CD Pack $19.95

Encyclopedia of Reading Rhythms
by Gary Hess • **Private Lessons**
00695145 . . . . $19.95

Going Pro
by Kenny Kerner • **Private Lessons**
00695322 . . . . $17.95

Harmony & Theory
by Keith Wyatt & Carl Schroeder • **Essential Concepts**
00695161 . . . . $17.95

Home Recording Basics
featuring Dallan Beck
00695655 VHS Video $19.95

Lead Sheet Bible
by Robin Randall & Janice Peterson • **Private Lessons**
00695130 Book/CD Pack $19.95

FOR MORE INFORMATION, SEE YOUR LOCAL MUSIC DEALER, OR WRITE TO:

HAL•LEONARD®
CORPORATION
7777 W. BLUEMOUND RD. P.O. BOX 13819 MILWAUKEE, WI 53213
Visit Hal Leonard Online at **www.halleonard.com**

Prices, contents, and availability subject to change without notice

0705